insight text guide

Iain Sinclair

Death of a Salesman

Arthur Miller

Copyright © Insight Publications 2011

First published in 2011, reprinted in 2012, 2013, 2015 (twice), 2016, 2019, 2020, 2021.

Insight Publications Pty Ltd
3/350 Charman Road
Cheltenham VIC 3192
Australia
Tel: +61 3 8571 4950
Fax: +61 3 8571 0257
Email: books@insightpublications.com.au

www.insightpublications.com.au

Copying for educational purposes
The Australian *Copyright Act 1968* (the Act) allows a maximum of one chapter or 10% of this book, whichever is the greater, to be copied by any educational institution for its educational purposes provided that the educational institution (or the body that administers it) has given a remuneration notice to Copyright Agency under the Act.

For details of the Copyright Agency licence for educational institutions contact:

Copyright Agency
Tel: +61 2 9394 7600
Fax: +61 2 9394 7601
www.copyright.com.au

Copying for other purposes
Except as permitted under the Act (for example, any fair dealing for the purposes of study, research, criticism or review) no part of this book may be reproduced, stored in a retrieval system, or transmitted in any form or by any means without prior written permission. All inquiries should be made to the publisher at the address above.

National Library of Australia Cataloguing-in-Publication entry:
Sinclair, Iain.
Arthur Miller's death of a salesman / Iain Sinclair.
9781921411830 (pbk.)
For secondary school age.
Miller, Arthur, 1915-2005 Death of a salesman.
Miller, Arthur, 1915-2005--Criticism and interpretation.
812.52

Other ISBNs:
9781925175080 (digital)
9781925175417 (bundle: print + digital)

Cover design: The Modern Art Production Group

Printed in Australia by Ligare

contents

CHARACTER MAP

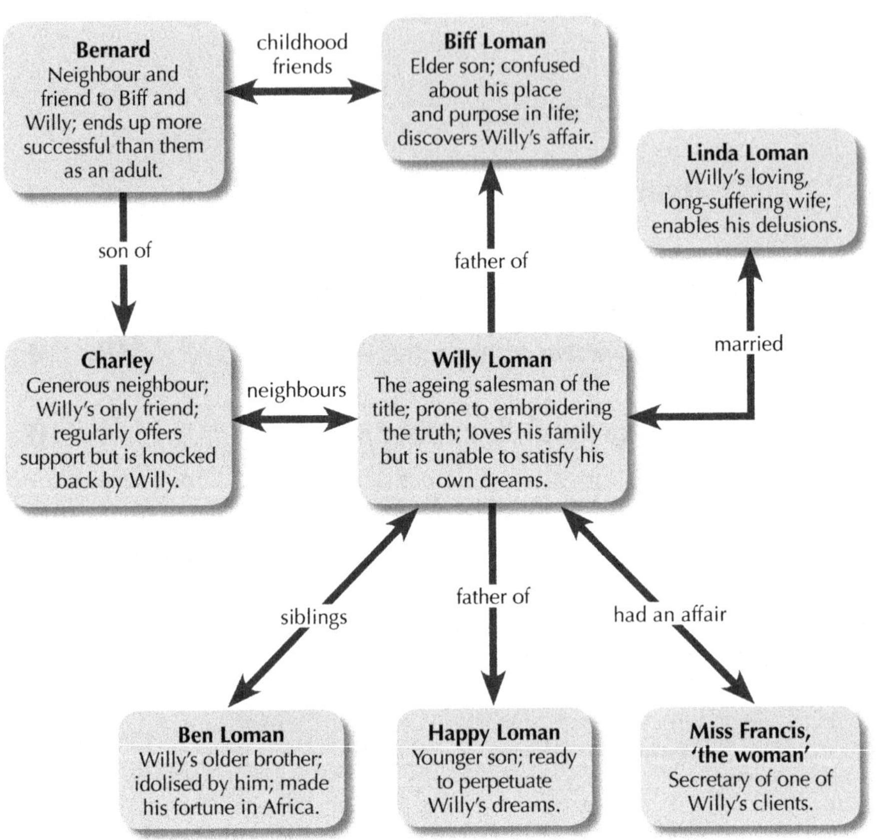

OVERVIEW

About the author

Arthur Miller is best known as a first-class dramatist who exposed his nation's Achilles heels, and as a navigator of America's national psyche. His greatest work, *Death of a Salesman* (1949), created its own genre: the American tragedy. American tragedy spotlights the weakest links in the great American Dream, and reminds us of its finest aspirations. *Death of a Salesman* reveals that most ordinary people are unable to achieve the American Dream, no matter how much they believe in it or how hard they work. Miller's other great work, *The Crucible* (1953), reveals the restrictions imposed on individual freedom in 'the land of the free'. He is a playwright who uncovered the contradictions in his own society while appealing to its core values. He introduced the thinking of Sigmund Freud and Carl Jung to dramatic writing in America, stripped bare the illusions of a nation and also married its most famous sweetheart, Marilyn Monroe.

Born on 17 October 1915 into a lower-middle-class Jewish family in Manhattan, New York, Arthur Miller was an unremarkable high school student. He paid his own way through a Bachelor of Arts degree at the University of Michigan in 1938 and had his first play, *The Man Who Had All the Luck*, published in 1944; it was extremely well received and he quickly moved on to success as a writer. In 1947, Miller's first major play success, *All My Sons*, laid the foundations for his next play, *Death of a Salesman*, which would cause a national sensation. This was a Pulitzer Prize winner: a play critiquing the social and philosophical failings of capitalism, and the cost of blind faith in the American Dream.

The lead character in *Death of a Salesman* is Willy Loman, a failing door-to-door salesman coming to the end of his life but doggedly holding on to lost dreams. Willy was modelled on Miller's own uncle, a man called Manny Newman, who insisted on maintaining the appearance of complete confidence coupled with a point-blank refusal to countenance failure of any kind. The playwright combined these real-life qualities of his uncle (a regular American man) with mythic principles drawn from ancient Greek theatre. American tragedy explores the great myths that govern a society by examining the lives of its most ordinary citizens.

Before American tragedy, a society's myths were examined in tragedy through its kings and great heroes. In ancient Greece, Sophocles' *Oedipus Cycle* was a trilogy of plays about a king, while *Death of a Salesman* is about a poor door-to-door salesman. The important factor to remember with American tragedy is that the scale of the drama is as large as the Greeks' but instead of dealing with the lives of gods or kings, the subject matter is everyday people. *Death of a Salesman* is far more than just a tale of a man refusing to let go of his dreams in the face of certain failure; it is a play arguing that hollow materialism has come to replace the great ideals on which America was founded.

Arthur Miller's other major work, *The Crucible*, continues his mythic and tragic exploration of American values by drawing parallels between the treatment of those accused of witchcraft in the early days of the American colonies in the 1690s and those accused of communism in the 1950s. Again Miller focuses on the lives of ordinary Americans (this time those living in the 1690s in Salem, Massachusetts), and again has a very direct personal connection to the story. Arthur Miller was called before the House Un-American Activities Committee in 1956 and asked to name people thought to have been members of the illegal Communist Party. He refused to name anyone and was convicted of contempt of Congress in 1957 (the conviction was reversed by the Supreme Court in 1958). This political witch-hunt, known as 'McCarthyism' (after Senator Joseph McCarthy who led the committee) served as the basis for Miller to draw associations in his play with Americans who lived in a time when they were not protected by a bill of rights. Once again Miller used a small-scale personal story as the basis of a drama that tapped right into the consciousness of a whole nation.

Synopsis

Willy Loman is a travelling salesman at the end of his career. The beginning of the play sees him returning home to his wife Linda after nearly crashing his car. Biff and Happy, their adult sons, are on a rare trip home. The relationship between Biff and his father is strained. Willy thinks Biff is a 'lazy bum' (p.11): he has not found himself a career at the age of thirty-four. Upstairs in their bedroom, Biff talks to his brother,

Happy, about his own inability to settle and his anger at his father's criticism of him.

Alone in the kitchen, Willy retreats into his memory: remembering the boys as teenagers, imagining Biff being a top-class footballer and reliving conversations with his successful brother, Ben. Within these memories are also hints of where things started to go wrong for Willy – where he exaggerates his success, dismisses Biff's stealing and lies to his wife. The past and present continue to mingle in Willy's mind throughout a visit by his friend Charley, who offers him a job, which Willy proudly rejects. During the play, Willy frequently drifts in and out of the present, interacting with characters from his past.

The brothers and Linda discuss Willy – Linda defends him and attacks her sons for their treatment of him. She tells them of her fear that Willy is trying to kill himself. When Willy irritably rejoins them, Biff tries to placate him by saying he will go and see an old employer, Oliver, and ask for a job. This escalates into a plan for the brothers to set up a business together. Willy is delighted and the whole family is drawn into this daydream. At the end of the act, however, Biff finds a length of rubber tubing that Willy has hidden (to use to commit suicide).

The second act opens happily with Willy making plans to ask his boss for a desk job and then meet his sons for dinner. However, Willy's boss (Howard) will not give him a different job and, instead, tells Willy he is fired. This triggers Willy's memories of turning down his brother Ben's offer of a job. Willy then goes to Charley's office to borrow money and meets Charley's son Bernard, whom Willy had ridiculed as a boy but who is now a successful lawyer. Charley again offers him a job and Willy is again furious at being 'insulted' (p.76).

In the restaurant that evening, Biff tells Happy that Oliver did not remember him, leading him to realise he had been lying to himself about his importance in the company. As Biff left the office he stole a fountain pen. Willy enters and Biff tries to tell him what has happened but Willy won't listen. Biff and Happy leave Willy alone in the restroom, to go off for the night with two girls from the restaurant. Willy remembers an incident in Boston where Biff was devastated to discover him with a woman. On the boys' return to the house, Linda is furious, and Willy is talking to his absent brother Ben about his plan to commit suicide so his family can have the insurance money. Biff and Willy argue again and Biff tells his family that he has lost every job he ever had, through stealing, and that he has been in jail. However, Willy chooses to interpret Biff's breakdown and moment of tenderness in front of his father as proof that Biff still likes him. Willy decides that if he leaves Biff the money, Biff will be 'magnificent' (p.106). As the others go to bed, Willy leaves the house and, offstage, crashes his car.

In the 'Requiem' at the graveside, the family react in different ways – Happy is angry; Charley believes that a mismatch of temperament, job and dreams has destroyed Willy; Biff declares that Willy had 'the wrong dreams' (p.110). The scene ends with Linda left alone. She laments that Willy has given up at the exact point when they have just made the final payment on the house and are 'free and clear' (p.112).

Character summaries

Willy Loman

An ageing travelling salesman.

Linda Loman

Willy's wife.

Biff Loman

Willy's elder son.

Harold 'Happy' Loman

Willy's younger son.

Charley

Willy's neighbour and only friend.

Bernard

Charley's son, a friend and playmate of Biff's; looks up to Biff even though Biff takes advantage of him; now a successful lawyer.

Jenny

Charley's secretary.

Ben

Willy's older brother; idolised by Willy; recently died in Africa, but Willy regularly interacts with him during the play.

Howard Wagner

Willy's boss; his father before him was Willy's boss when Howard was born; often represented by critics as the heartless face of capitalism and progress.

Miss Francis

Also called 'The Woman'; secretary to one of Willy's clients in Boston; has an affair with Willy and represents the destruction of Biff's faith in both Willy and himself.

Letta and Miss Forsythe

Prostitutes in Frank's Chop House.

Stanley and a Waiter

Waiters in Frank's Chop House.

BACKGROUND & CONTEXT

Historical, economic and social context

The historical context of *Death of a Salesman* is very important. As a social drama, much of the play resonates with and comments on aspects of society at that time. Consider, for example, the economic situation in America in 1949. Following a considerable period of lean times brought on by the Great Depression and then the Second World War, America experienced an unprecedented period of economic growth. The country had been geared up for massive industrial production during the war, and peacetime directed that industrial potential onto the domestic market. For the first time in nearly thirty years there was a surplus of goods, from foodstuffs to electronics to cars, and a good deal of money going around with which to buy them. Large-scale housing (especially construction of urban apartment blocks) and inner-city businesses experienced a boom.

The boom of the late 1940s, however, didn't bring prosperity to everyone. The massive amount of people buying goods triggered inflation and many normal Americans on moderate wages suddenly found themselves unable to afford a lot of products. Small-scale farmers also experienced difficulties because the American government had embarked on a series of policies designed to encourage mass food production by large corporations. It was a time when big business started to thrive at the expense of the individual operator.

The first workers to be hit hard by this change in the economic situation were the lowest-paid, unskilled workers like field labourers, shop clerks, janitors (cleaners), waiters and salesmen. In the play, Biff has been working as a field labourer for a small-scale farmer and Happy is an assistant to the assistant clerk in a clothing store. Both of these kinds of workers would have experienced a significant reduction in their wages and spending power. At the same time, other members of American society (shareholders, professionals, businessmen, middle management) would have been enjoying the benefits of a massive boost in corporate earnings. The rich started getting richer while the poor started getting poorer – a trend that has continued in America to this day.

Another significant change in the economic situation was an increase in the use of credit, which triggered more inflation. Cash-rich corporations encouraged customers to use credit to buy products at inflated prices that they could not normally afford. People used credit to buy commodity items like cars and houses. There is evidence in *Death of a Salesman* that Willy has relied heavily on credit, as we see the pressures of his repayments restricting his ability to afford basic domestic necessities.

The global political climate was also an important factor. America was in the early stages of the Cold War with their new ideological enemies, the Soviet Union. In order to prove their ideological and economic superiority, American citizens started to feel obliged to exercise their democratic right to freedom and prosperity by diving headfirst into capitalism and materialism. The acquisition of goods and ostentatious demonstrations of affluence moved a notch up the social ladder and was widely deemed to be an act of patriotism. Being rich and owning advanced technology was physical proof that the 'American Dream' of freedom and opportunity was morally and materially superior to Communism's dictum of 'From each according to his ability, to each according to his needs'. Personal and national pride had become fused together and the acquisition of wealth had become an explicit and requisite expression of 'freedom and liberty'.

Notice also that there are in fact two versions of the great American Dream being alluded to. There is Willy's, which is distinctively urban – focused on money and materials – and Biff and Ben's, with a 'go West, young man' mythology belonging to the century before. This second dream was founded on adventure, physical endeavour and claiming a birthright – the kinds of values embodied in 'Western' movies.

Author's historical context

Arthur Miller's father, Isidore, had originally owned his own business as a manufacturer of ladieswear but had lost everything during the Great Depression. He went on to life as a shopkeeper and his family experienced a transformation – from being beneficiaries of the new American prosperity to finding themselves low-wage earners in a time when only businesses and shareholders were really doing well. Miller recalls his father being deeply saddened that he could not pass his business down to the boys.

Throughout his education, Miller had to work to earn his keep. At school, he played football and was a poor to mediocre student. Some of these parallels with the play are striking. Miller states that he came up with the concept for *Death of a Salesman* at age seventeen while working for his father. After seeing firsthand the kind of pressure that travelling salesmen working on commission were under, he wrote a short story about a salesman who is ridiculed by his colleagues and ultimately throws himself under a train. This idea lay undeveloped until Miller was inspired by his uncle, Manny Newman. Manny was a salesman with a strong competitive streak and a very wilful personality who was known to compete fiercely with his two sons, Buddy and Abby. Manny's son Buddy (like Biff) was a very popular sportsman at school but did not live up to his potential – the similarities again are notable. Miller's *All My Sons* also deals with two sons who have a complicated relationship with their father. This theme of fathers desperate to pass on their dreams to unreceptive or unable sons seems linked to Miller's personal history.

The critic CWE Bigsby said of Miller that he saw salesmen 'like artists, like actors whose product is first of all themselves, forever imagining triumphs in a world that either ignores them or denies their presence altogether. But just often enough to keep the game going one of them makes it and swings to the moon on a thread of dreams unwinding out of himself' (in Miller 1978, p.127).

GENRE, STRUCTURE & LANGUAGE

Genre

> The form of *Death of a Salesman* was an attempt, as much as anything else, to convey the bending of time. There are two or three sorts of time in the play. One is social time; one is psychic time, the way we remember things; and the third one is the sense of time created by the play and shared by the audience ... The play is taking place in ... 24 hours; and yet it is dealing with material that goes back probably 25 years. (Miller, cited in Roudané 1987, p.370)

A genre is a type, class or variety of something. It is a French word derived from the Latin *genus*. In a literary and dramatic sense, genre refers to a body of work that shares similarities in structure, language or subject matter. Using the idea of genre can be a useful tool because it provides us with a framework to make specific observations about a piece of art. In music, for example, we are able to evaluate work because we understand the underlying rules of different genres like rock, country, indie, jazz or classical. Drama can also be divided into genres: a short list would include ***classical tragedy***, ***classical comedy***, ***commedia dell'arte***, ***tragicomedy***, ***melodrama***, ***Sturm und Drang***, ***comedy of manners*** and, in recent times, the ***well-made play***, ***realism***, ***social realism***, ***magic realism***, ***kitchen-sink drama*** and many, many more.

Death of a Salesman is interesting because while it clearly belongs to a specific genre (tragedy) it also makes liberal use of techniques from a number of different dramatic styles. This mixed and complicated version of tragedy is sometimes called 'American' or 'modern' tragedy.

In Miller's description of the play, he talks about conveying 'the bending of time' and indeed the play uses structural techniques that allow for a fluid change in timeframes without any significant disruption to the dramatic action. Notice how, early in Act One, Willy switches from talking to his wife Linda in 'real time' to speaking with his projected memories of Biff and Happy and then The Woman and straight back to

Linda again in a seamless flow. This kind of technique belongs to a genre known as ***expressionism***, yet at other times the play recreates scenes in a manner so natural and precise that they must be examples of ***social realism***. *Death of a Salesman* could also be said to belong to a genre that emerged after the Second World War: the American ***memory play***, where the internal world of the protagonist, and of course their memories, make up the bulk of the dramatic action. The most prolific and recognised proponent of the memory play was Tennessee Williams, with his *The Glass Menagerie* being the most famous example of the genre.

Structure

> Writing in that form was like moving through a corridor in a dream, knowing instinctively that one would find every wriggle of it and, best of all, where the exit lay. There is something like a dream's quality in my memory of the writing and the day or two that followed its completion. (Miller 1950)

It is useful to think of the structure of *Death of a Salesman* in relation to the structure of dreams. We often experience dreams as a seamless narrative – that is, a story that feels continuous and connected – and yet when we try to relate that story to someone else we realise that in fact the dream consists of extraordinary and often incredible leaps in space, time and even logic. *Death of a Salesman* functions in a similar way, with the key difference being that the dream experience belongs to Willy Loman and we are witnessing it from the outside. Before Arthur Miller decided on the final title, the play was actually called *The Inside of his Head*. When you think about structure in this play, what you are actually thinking about is Miller's own attempt to dramatise another human being's internal psychological workings. Some critics refer to the play as being driven by 'flashbacks' but on closer examination we can see that, unlike a flashback (where the play jumps back in time) what actually happens is a psychologically-driven 'mixed reality'. (For example, even though Willy may be talking to a teenage Biff, we are very much aware that Willy is still drinking a glass of milk in his kitchen in the present time). The English director Richard Eyre describes the realities in *Death of a Salesman* as 'co-existing in a compound metaphor' (2003). Rather than thinking of the moments in the past as 'flashbacks', try thinking of them as psychological 'projections' triggered by experiences happening in the present time. Flashbacks are usually fixed versions of the past recreated to provide insight on current events, but Willy's experiences are different. They seem to change and interact with what is occurring in the present. Eyre's idea of the different realities co-existing is a very useful way of interpreting the structure of the piece.

While the mechanism of the scenes and the seamless switching between timeframes or versions of reality was very innovative for its era, the broader structure of the play is very old fashioned. The play is divided into three acts: this was the most common form for plays written in the nineteenth and twentieth centuries. In Miller's play we are presented with Act One, Act Two and a 'Requiem'. The play's full title is: *Death of a Salesman: Certain Private Conversations in Two Acts and a Requiem*. The practice of referring to the structure of a play in its title was common in the sixteenth, seventeenth and eighteenth century, but by the late twentieth century had become quite unusual. It seems that Miller was attempting a radically new internal structure while also framing the play using a traditional, well-known pattern common to the genre. This allows the play to feel modern and intensely personal, while at the same time retaining a classic and enduring tone. The play is given both a 'private' and an 'epic' dimension as a result.

Language

The style of language generally used by the characters is what is called 'demotic'. When language is 'demotic' it means that characters sound like everyday people from the specific place in time to which they belong. The word comes from the ancient Greek *demotikos*, meaning 'of the common people'. All of the characters speak with a common touch that is unmistakably early postwar, working class Brooklyn. It is perhaps best represented in Biff's speech patterns, which sometimes contradict accepted grammar and can appear illogical to a reader, but when spoken and heard, the lines assume a whole new level of eloquence. Try reading the following line and then try speaking it aloud: 'I'm mixed up very bad.

Maybe I oughta get married. Maybe I oughta get stuck into something' (p.17). Demotic language nearly always has the feeling that it is being spoken from the heart (rather than the head). It is a language that has been written to be spoken.

While the dialogue is demotic, Miller also lets his characters use figurative language (words or expressions with a meaning beyond the literal). Other ways of describing this would be 'poetic' or 'grand'. Often the characters will slip into figurative language at times of high stress or strong emotional intensity. Miller uses this technique to elevate the sense of drama at the same time as increasing the general eloquence. Some examples include:

- when Linda accuses Biff of being flighty: 'a man is not a bird, to come and go with the springtime' (p.43)
- when Linda begs Biff on the phone saying, 'Be loving to him. Because he's only a little boat looking for a harbour' (p.59)
- when Willy begs Howard for a different job: 'You can't eat the orange and throw the peel away – a man is not a piece of fruit!' (p.64).

There are other times when the language is less poetic and more deliberately grand, such as when Charley speaks at Willy's grave and adopts a kind of faux religiosity: 'Nobody dast blame this man' (p.111). This has the same kind of epic feel as the words 'Lest we forget' (from Rudyard Kipling's poem, 'Recessional') – even though we don't use words like 'dast' and 'lest' in standard speech, when they are used at heightened moments of human experience they somehow seem to fit.

Arthur Miller had a great ear for the way real people use language, and can find the idiom for whatever place or time he sets his plays. Compare the language of *Death of a Salesman* to that employed in his other masterpiece, *The Crucible*, set in Salem in the 1690s, and you will notice that while they are very different in form and structure, the intensity and sense of realism in speech is palpable: 'A man may think God sleeps, but God sees everything, I know it now. I beg you, sir, I beg you – see her what she is … She thinks to dance with me on my wife's grave! And well she might, for I thought of her softly. God help me, I lusted, and there *is* a promise in such sweat. But it is a whore's vengeance …' (Miller 1953, p.98).

SCENE-BY-SCENE ANALYSIS

Arthur Miller breaks his play into two acts followed by a 'Requiem' but he does not mark out the scenes. In the scene-by-scene analysis here you will see that scene numbers have been added, to break up the text into useable chunks for analysis. When you refer to sections of the play in essays and exams, don't use these scene numbers: state the act and then the page number instead. For example, 'Biff: Pop! I'm a dime a dozen, and so are you!' (Act 2, p.105), and not 'Biff: Pop! I'm a dime a dozen, and so are you!' (Act 2, Scene 9).

Act 1, Scene 1 (pp.7–14)

Summary: *An ageing salesman returns home from work early.*

Our first experience in the play is hearing a flute, *'telling of grass and trees and the horizon'* (p.7). Flute music appears at very specific moments in the play. Next we see a small old house dwarfed by new apartment blocks surrounding it and after that we see a tired man of sixty-two (Willy) carrying large salesman's sample cases.

Key points

- When Linda talks to Willy about his early return she sugar-coats the way she speaks to him. In this first scene, we discover Willy's tendency to alter the truth of events to suit his purpose.
- Willy alters the truth the most when he talks of his work or his eldest son Biff (who has just returned home).
- Willy's mood is bright when he reminisces about the past and is very bleak or agitated in the present.
- Notice how the past and the present mix and mingle with each other.
- We see the forces of present life pressing hard on this ageing couple.

Q See if you can identify how often the truth is altered in this section. Why might that be?

Vocabulary:

Yonkers: A city just north of New York.

Act 1, Scene 2 (pp.14–20)

Summary: *Biff and Happy talk upstairs.*

In this scene we meet Willy and Linda's two sons; they both talk of their past happiness and current dissatisfaction.

Key points

- Biff is seeking a way to find order in his life while Happy is seeking ways of imposing disorder on others.
- Both boys demonstrate an image of themselves as attractive and physical.
- Biff believes their current unhappiness stems from the fact that they 'weren't brought up to grub for money' (p.18), for which he blames his father.
- Biff hints to Happy that something very specific has brought on this current sense of failure, but won't tell him outright.

Q Does the Biff you meet here match the Biff that Willy describes?

Act 1, Scene 3 (pp.20–4)

Summary: *Willy remembers polishing the Chevrolet along with his sons.*

This scene marks a significant shift in the style of the play. Until now the play has been mostly realistic (we have been in one time and place). Now Willy's daydreaming becomes tangible.

Key points

- We see what is going on inside Willy's imagination recreated on the stage. Willy is in the kitchen, during the 1950s, drinking a glass of milk on his own, but we are transported to the 1930s through his imagination.
- The characters we meet in this scene are 'projections' of Willy's imagination and are reflections of his subconscious.
- We see the seeds of Biff and Happy's discontent being sown. Biff is all but encouraged to cheat at school: his theft of a football is blithely overlooked and his offer to defy his coach's instructions triggers praise from Willy.

- Biff is desperate for his father's attention.
- Willy instils a belief in his sons that the world will reward them for their physical attractiveness. They are taught to expect that different rules will apply to them.

> ***Q*** Do you think Willy's parenting is responsible? Is Willy interested in his son's upbringing or in his own feelings?

Vocabulary:

Gene Tunney: Irish-American world heavyweight boxing champion from 1926 to 1928.

Simonize: To polish and care for.

Act 1, Scene 4 (pp.24–6)

Summary: *Bernard appears from next door.*

The boy from next door, Bernard, intrudes on Willy's daydream. He is here to warn Biff that he is danger of failing his math exams (and therefore losing his chance of a scholarship to university). Willy hears this but shrugs off the gravity of the situation and is easily distracted by Biff showing him a hand-drawn University of Virginia logo on his sneakers.

Key point

Notice how harsh Willy is with Bernard – how certain he is that Bernard will not get far in life – and how much he revels in his belief in his own son's popularity at school.

> ***Q*** Why does Willy shrug off such serious issues? The scene seems to emerge from Willy's subconscious: what does this tell us about Willy himself?

Vocabulary:

Adonis: A beautiful and athletic man; character in ancient Greek legend.

Act 1, Scene 5 (pp.26–9)

Summary: *Complications arise as the truth seeps in.*

In this scene the boys join their many friends doing chores in the cellar. Willy and Linda discuss domestic matters and a strange woman intrudes. We are presented with a portrait of a man unwilling to deal with things as they are. This scene gives us a firsthand experience of Willy changing his reality to suit the needs of his ego.

Key points

- The scene begins in Willy's daydream about his sons, eighteen years ago, but the realities start to fragment, taking us from the daydream into a memory of another woman.
- Willy gets agitated very quickly when faced with reality. Watch how willing he is to reframe his perception of the world depending on his needs, such as when he downgrades the size of his commission.

Q Do you think Willy is delusional or is something else going on? Is there evidence of Willy knowingly changing the truth?

Act 1, Scene 6 (pp.29–32)

Summary: *Willy's mistress appears; Willy's illusions collapse back into the unpleasant reality.*

Once again a character intrudes on Willy's version of reality – this time we are transported to a Boston hotel room where he is with his mistress, Miss Francis. This scene is important because we can see that Willy is not in control of his imaginings and that he is unable to prevent dark undercurrents from leaking out. We also see what other people see when Willy becomes reminiscent.

After a time, when Willy's mind comes back to the present, he sees Linda again. Still caught between the two worlds he confuses her by saying 'I'll make it all up to you' (p.30), revealing his great sense of guilt.

Key points

- Willy has difficulty differentiating where his is, between the imagined Miss Francis and his own wife in the present moment. The realities blur and blend so much at the end of this scene that Linda leaves confused and in tears.
- Notice the motif of the stockings; Willy's guilt makes a connection between the stockings he gave his mistress and the ones Linda is currently mending.
- When Willy notices Linda mending her stocking the associations are too strong. He has an outburst of anger and suddenly his carefully constructed illusions about Biff collapse in a heap around him.

Q Can you think of a time when your own feelings have triggered a strong memory? What kinds of emotions trigger powerful memories?

Q Why does Linda run from the room?

Vocabulary:

Regents: Compulsory high school examinations in the state of New York.

Act 1, Scene 7 (pp.32–4)

Summary: *Happy and Charley check in on Willy; Willy's brother Ben appears.*

Willy finds himself alone for a short moment after Linda leaves; he tries to convince himself that he only taught his sons 'decent things' (p.32). Charley drops by to play cards (presumably as a way of calming Willy down), but Willy can't keep his mind on the cards and slips into another imagining, this time with his elder brother Ben.

Key points

- Ben (or at least Willy's projection of him) will make a number of appearances from now on. Each time Ben appears it is at a high point of Willy's confusion and distress.

- In this scene we see Willy maintaining a dual conversation in two different realities. Charley of course does not see Ben, but he sees Willy talking to thin air. By seeing Charley's behaviour we can infer that Willy is not simply 'remembering' something: he is interacting with his hallucination.
- Willy takes Charley's job offer as an insult. In later scenes when we see Willy begging to keep his job, we will understand that it is less about money than it is about his identity as a salesman.

Q Why do you think Willy is so tough on Charley? Does he deserve the treatment Willy metes out?

Act 1, Scene 8 (pp.34–9)

Summary: *Ben makes a surprise visit to the young Loman family.*

Willy recreates a day when his estranged brother Ben turns up out of the blue. Ben hardly knows his brother, having left to follow his father when Willy was very young. However, Ben provides us with some clues about Willy's upbringing. The family travelled across America in a wagon and would often camp around a fire telling stories; their father (like Ben) was 'wild-hearted' (p.38). Willy tries hard to gain approval from Ben in this scene, but there is a hypocritical inconsistency in that Willy idolises Ben for his adventurous spirit but is fiercely critical of Biff's desires to go out West and to become a carpenter or a cowboy.

Willy's daydream is broken at the end of this scene, by a watchman who catches young Biff and Happy stealing sand from a construction site on Willy's orders.

Key points

- We can assume from the information in this scene that Willy was brought up mainly by his mother. Keep this in mind in relation to Willy's 'abandonment complex' (discussed in 'Characters and Relationships').
- Remember that Ben is a 'projection' or construct of Willy's imagination; read the scene again and you will notice that the images Ben creates are classic images of exploration and the 'Old West'. Notice Willy's desperate attempts to impress Ben and connect himself to the idea of a pioneering family.

Q Is it strange that Ben was headed for Alaska but then arrived in Africa? What evidence is there to suggest that much of what Ben says is invented?

Vocabulary:

Alaska: The northernmost American state.

The Gold Coast: The coast of West Africa.

Ketchikan: A city in Alaska.

Act 1, Scene 9 (pp.39–48)

Summary: *Linda tells Biff some sobering news.*

After Willy has gone upstairs, Biff comes down into the kitchen to talk with his mother. Linda speaks with a different voice when Willy is not around. This scene is important because we see Linda in a different light and discover why she works so desperately to prop up Willy's delusions; she believes (correctly) that Willy is on the verge of suicide.

Key points

- We see the weight and complexity of Linda's burden: she is aware of the full truth but is repeatedly and increasingly forced to fake it (yet she ignores Biff calling Willy 'a fake', p.45). She knowingly sugar-coats the truth because she finds Willy's suffering unbearable.
- Linda gives a clear assessment of Biff and Happy's characters. It is very different to the fiction she allows Willy to believe.

Q Many of us tell 'white lies' from time to time. Where do you draw the line between a white lie and an unacceptable deception?

Act 1, Scene 10 (pp.48–54)

Summary: *Willy and Biff start to fight, then form an entente.*

An entente is an informal understanding that brings peace. In this scene Biff relaxes his harsh position toward his father because of news of his illness. When Willy reappears, Biff adopts a conciliatory tone and Linda shifts her manner and tone in front of Willy. Between them, they allow Willy to reclaim a dominant position and a sense of order settles on the house. But when Willy is harsh with Linda, Biff becomes protective and assumes a dominant role again, threatening the calm. As always, Linda and Happy maintain order by allowing manipulation of the truth to keep Willy calm.

Key points

- Biff tries to start an honest conversation but Willy rejects him, cutting him off and dominating the direction of conversation until the entente is almost broken.
- We can see that Biff will not be able to play the status game for long. Willy goes to bed feeling that he has the high status, because Biff has allowed him to feel that way. As the act concludes, Willy sleeps wrapped in a delusion that all will be well the next day.

Vocabulary:

Ebbets Field: A Major League Baseball park in Brooklyn, New York.

Act 2, Scene 1 (pp.55–9)

Summary: *Willy and Linda share a breakfast full of promise.*

The opening scene of the second act in most plays carries a very strong energy. This is because the playwright needs to pull the audience back into the world of the play when they return from the interval. In *Death of a Salesman*, this scene also has a very different feel to most of the play. The key difference is in Willy; there is none of the usual exaggeration and manipulation of the truth or digression into the past. There's a sense that this is what Willy used to be like and the scene offers an insight into how good Linda and Willy's relationship once was. Of course, a number of the reasons why Willy feels so good are falsely manufactured for his benefit, but for a brief moment we are given a chance to meet the man that Linda fell in love with.

Key points

- There are signs that the happiness will be short-lived; Willy becomes agitated when Linda reminds him that there are extra household costs to attend to.
- Note the irony of Willy complaining about products being timed to break down just as they are paid off – salesmen often rely on that very mechanism.
- Seeds are introduced as a symbol of new beginning.
- We discover that a large reason for Linda's optimism is that she believes Willy has removed a rubber hose he had attached to the gas system to asphyxiate himself.
- When Biff tells her that he removed the pipe Linda remains buoyant, but her deep worry is betrayed by her line 'he's only a little boat looking for a harbour ... you'll save his life' (p.59).

Q Could Willy's optimism hinge on his hope that Biff has forgiven him for what happened in Boston? What other reasons might he have for this optimism?

Act 2, Scene 2 (pp.59–66)

Summary: *Willy meets with his boss Howard about getting a job in the city.*

Until now the play has been set in Willy's house. Each of Willy's daydreams has reverted back to his home. This scene breaks away from the house and ends on the streets of Manhattan. Willy's location now changes with each place he visits. Once Willy is fired he is left with no connection to his identity and he starts to fall into uncontrolled delusions.

Key points

- When we meet Howard he is playing with a new piece of technology that records voices. Willy tries to divert Howard's attention to his stories but does not stand a chance against this novelty. Willy uses all of his sales magic and yet is defeated by an inanimate object: a potent image of the future.

- For a boss with 'a line of people to see' (p.66), Howard seems to give Willy a good deal of time and is clearly respectful towards him. He even tolerates Willy's long monologue of stories about his past and his dreams (pp.63–4).
- There is a strong suggestion that Howard has been suffering Willy's erratic behaviour for some time and it is only when Willy's behaviour becomes extreme that Howard decides to fire Willy from the company.
- Observe Willy's pattern of reverting to the past when things don't go his way: first by bringing up Howard's father and Willy's own role in Howard's naming, then by reminiscing about the legendary Dave Singleman, a salesman who died on the job at the age of eighty-four.

Q Is Howard a heartless man, or are we seeing a man who has become immune to Willy's words and who now has to protect his company from an unstable representative?

Act 2, Scene 3 (pp.66–8)

Summary: *Ben makes Willy an offer for the future.*

In a moment of great crisis Willy once again reverts to a memory of Ben. This time Ben makes a concrete offer for Willy and the boys to join him in Alaska. Willy is attracted to the proposition and presents the case to Linda. Linda, however, is against the idea and gives strong arguments why Willy should stay in New York.

Key point

While Ben remains in his base reality in the past, Willy seems to talk to Ben in a blend of both the past and the present, asking for advice in both time streams.

Q If we keep in mind that Linda is a projection from Willy's imagination here, do you think Willy's subconscious mind is blaming Linda for missing the opportunity of a lifetime?

Act 2, Scene 4 (pp.68–78)

Summary: *Bernard questions Willy about the change in Biff; Charley extends an offer of help to Willy.*

The scene begins in a memory of the past, with the boys getting ready to go to the big game at Ebbets Field, but quickly shifts to the present, with Willy in the waiting room of Charley's business. In Charley's office we meet Bernard as an adult. He is strikingly different to Willy's remembered versions we met in the past (including a moment earlier, when both Bernard and Charley featured in Willy's memory).

The adult Bernard articulates an underlying and as-yet unanswered question of the play: What happened when Biff went to visit Willy in Boston (p.74)? Miller has been ***foreshadowing*** or ***prefiguring*** this big question being asked. We have seen the mistress in Act One and have noticed Biff bring up and then drop the subject a number of times. As Bernard pushes Willy closer to the truth about what happened, the stage directions note that Willy '*looks at him as at an intruder*' (p.74).

Key points

- Bernard is carrying tennis rackets. Sport was a domain from which Bernard was previously excluded, but now Bernard has surpassed Biff on every level.
- A significant shift occurs in Willy's character. Up until now we have seen Willy actively eluding difficult elements of his life, but now in his weakened and desperate state he asks where he might have gone wrong.
- This scene is important because we see Willy reject another job offer from Charley even though he has just been fired; this indicates that Willy's money problems come a very pale second to his pride and to his identity as a salesman.
- Note the contrast between Charley's appraisal of being a salesman and the heroic portrait Willy drew earlier of Dave Singleman.
- The possibility of Willy's suicide has been prefigured a number of times in the play; Willy again hints at it here – 'you end up worth more dead than alive' (p.77) – and the danger comes freshly to our minds.

Act 2, Scene 5 (pp.78–83)

Summary: *Biff and Happy wait for Willy at Frank's Chop House.*

With our worries for Willy freshly renewed the play jumps to Frank's Chop House. The plan was for the three men to meet after work to celebrate each other's accomplishments. We already know about Willy's unsuccessful outcomes and now discover that Biff's are much the same with a key difference: Biff appears to have already made peace with his own failure.

Key points

- Happy's version of chasing success is seen in his overtures to the women in this scene.
- We are starting to come closer to the truth. Willy's subconscious knowledge of what happened to Biff is beginning to push through to the surface and his conscious acknowledgement of the damage he did is about to emerge as a ***cathartic realisation***.

Vocabulary:

Strudel: A nickname for a loose woman or prostitute.

Act 2, Scene 6 (pp.83–96)

Summary: *Biff visits Willy in Boston (past) and Willy is abandoned at the restaurant (present).*

The play has been building up to this scene from the moment Biff made the comment 'There's one or two other things depressing him, Happy' (p.16), through the appearance of the woman in the second daydream, the numerous times that Biff has almost raised the subject and of course Bernard's questioning of Willy about the moment where Biff had 'given up his life' (p.74).

We find ourselves in a hotel room in Boston. Willy is entertaining his mistress when Biff arrives to tell his father that he has failed his math exam. This is not news to the audience: Biff's exam failure has already been mentioned in Willy's memories. One symbolic way of looking at the many references to the news is that Willy's subconscious has been knocking on the door of the truth and this scene is the moment when he answers it – literally, when Biff knocks on the hotel door.

This is the moment Biff discovers his father's affair and all of his illusions shatter. We see that Biff's faith in himself had been inextricably bound to his faith in his own father and the collapse of one means the collapse of both. Biff calls his father a 'phony little fake' (p.95) and the scene is done. Willy can no longer suppress the memory and full knowledge that he alone is responsible for the failure of his son.

Key points

- When Willy arrives in the restaurant he refuses to receive Biff's bad news and falls into another daydream almost instantly. This time the daydream is dominated by the young Bernard intruding to pass on the news that 'Biff flunked math' (p.87).
- The realities begin to overlap as Willy speaks to the boys in the restaurant but also retreats into the memory of Boston. There is a strong sense that Willy is less and less in control of the memories taking hold of his consciousness; he is no longer able to select and manipulate his memories at will.
- When Willy returns to reality he discovers that the boys – one son who publicly disowned him and another who has no faith or respect in him – have left him to go out with the callgirls.
- Willy tells the waiter that he needs to buy seeds because he doesn't 'have a thing in the ground' (p.96). The symbolism of an old man abandoned in the city, asking where to buy seeds late in the evening, is powerful.

Vocabulary:

Chippie: A slang term for a loose woman or prostitute.

Act 2, Scene 7 (pp.96–9)

Summary: *Linda chastises her sons for abandoning Willy in the restaurant.*

Back at Willy's house in Brooklyn, Willy has been home for some time and Linda confronts her two sons for abandoning their own father on what was supposed to be a special night. Linda's treatment of the boys may seem harsh until we consider her deep concern for her husband's wellbeing and her disgust for her own sons' behaviour on a night that she had hoped would literally save Willy's life.

Key point

Once again, away from Willy, Linda presents a powerful force.

Act 2, Scene 8 (pp.99–101)

Summary: *Willy plants seeds; speaks to Ben about the possibility of suicide.*

Despite the fact that all of Willy's illusions have been laid to waste, we still see a man desperately searching for a silver lining. Willy finds one through the bleakest of thoughts. A few scenes ago Willy mused to Charley that a man is worth more dead than alive and the seeds of this dark thought start to take root. Speaking with Ben in the garden, he weighs up the benefits of killing himself (in order to leave his family the insurance money). Ben warns Willy that his plan may not succeed and that Biff is likely to think of his father as a dishonest coward.

Key point

We have been told that the garden no longer gets any sunlight because of urban development: the symbolism of a man planting seeds here is significant.

Act 2, Scene 9 (pp.101–9)

Summary: *Biff tries to level with his father one last time.*

Biff comes out into the garden to tell his father that he is leaving to go out West and that he has made peace with their differences. Willy refuses to stand in front of Linda with Biff. We see Willy's motive for suicide may not be completely altruistic and that his shame and guilt toward Linda is something from which he can no longer escape.

Up until now the truth has only emerged very occasionally – in the form of hints, moments of clarity at times of emotional distress or intrusions into dreams. Now Biff confronts his father's habitual dishonesty with an all-out truthful assault.

Willy becomes agitated and unpleasant when confronted with the truth but his defences are so weakened now that he can barely retaliate. Biff continues until he is exhausted. In this scene we witness two opposing forces (the absolute desire for the truth to come out and the absolute necessity for it to remain hidden) spending themselves out on each other. There is no sense of victory, merely a sense of stalemate.

Afterwards Willy entreats his family to go upstairs to bed. Talking to Ben again, Willy falls back into one final daydream: training his son to be a football star. Ben reminds Willy of the twenty-thousand-dollar life insurance policy. Linda calls out to Willy as the boys wait for him upstairs, but instead Willy climbs into his car and we hear him drive it off at speed. We hear a cacophony of music and then a single note of a cello (not a flute) pulsing and then coming to a stop.

Key points

- This scene is the key to the whole play and brings the two opposing forces of truth and lies together in open combat.
- There is a rare moment of tenderness between father and son, but even then Willy's compulsion to sugar-coat the truth comes out. Biff begs his father to 'take that phony dream and burn it before something happens'; his father's almost automatic and nonsensical response is 'he likes me!' (p.106).

- Willy's final words aren't even words: very poignant for a man who had based his life on (and ruined it with) a continuous and artful use of words. Flicking the ghosts of his final delusions away, he merely says 'Sh! ... Sh! Sh! ... Shhh!' (p.108).

Act 2, Scene 10 (pp.110–12), 'Requiem'

A requiem is a song or prayer dedicated to someone who has died. We see the Loman family standing with Charley at Willy's grave and discover that no one else has come to the funeral of the man who declared himself to be so 'well liked'. Only at the end of the requiem do we hear the flute come in, as it did in the beginning. As the play concludes, Linda is left alone in front of Willy's grave.

Key points

- Now that Willy is dead there is no longer any requirement to uphold lies; only Happy tries weakly (and in vain) to keep Willy's false dreams alive.
- Note how Charley (the only one capable of lending Willy some dignity) relies on a quasi-religious form of speech: 'Nobody dast blame this man' (p.111).
- This is the second 'death of a salesman' in the play. The first was the mythic idealised one of Dave Singleman, a man from the generation before who died respected and 'well liked'. Willy, the next generation on, dies discarded and forgotten.
- For the rest of the family it appears that Willy's final act has had the opposite effect to what was intended. They do not receive any money from the insurance and Willy is not seen as a hero.
- Willy's final act reveals that same flaw which has troubled his thinking all along: believing in dreams and ideas that have no basis in reality.
- The family experiences no resolution or reward from Willy's idea for salvation – only sadness, confusion and loss.

CHARACTERS & RELATIONSHIPS

Willy Loman

Key quotes

'I'm the New England man. I'm vital in New England' (p.10).

'...before it's all over we're gonna get a little place out in the country, and I'll raise some vegetables, a couple of chickens ...' (p.56).

'After all the highways, and the trains, and the appointments, and the years, you end up worth more dead than alive' (p.77).

> Willy's writing his name in a cake of ice on a hot day, but he wishes he were writing in stone. (Miller, in Kakutani 1984)

Willy is the protagonist and key tragic figure in *Death of a Salesman*. His life is also the central argument of the play. In fact, almost half of the characters we meet in the play are projections from Willy's own imagination. In this way Willy Loman joins a tradition of plays where a flawed central character's fortunes reflect profoundly on all other aspects of the play (examples include Joan of Arc, Don Quixote, King Lear, Hamlet, Job and King Oedipus). Critics have often called Willy Loman the first 'modern American tragic hero'. Modern heroes nearly always differ from classical heroes in one key area, and Willy Loman is no exception. In classical and Renaissance plays, the central character or hero experiences what the ancient Greeks called *peripeteia*: a colossal reversal of fortune from good to bad. This sets him on a course leading to a realisation that his downfall has been caused by his flaws and errors in judgment – such a realisation is called *anagnorisis*. In modern drama, central characters usually experience peripeteia but very often die (or solve their problem) before they get to a point of anagnorisis.

A question that has divided critics is whether Willy is wholly responsible for his reversal of fortune or if the world (and postwar American society in particular) has failed a decent, hardworking man. Of course the two positions are not mutually exclusive, and Miller's text supports arguments for each.

We are encouraged to think of Willy as an archetype (something representative of all other members of a particular category; Dracula, for example, can be seen as an archetype for all other vampires). Willy's name seems to have archetypal significance. He is a man low on the ladder of capitalism and who has a fiercely strong will, hence 'Will-y Lo(w)-man'. Many other character names in *Death of a Salesman* also have second meanings. For example, the almost mythical salesman on whom Willy tries to model himself is called 'Dave Singleman': a 'single' 'man' who stands out from the many.

Q If Willy is an archetype representing hardworking American people, why has his life ended in failure? Is it Willy's fault that he believed too fiercely in a dream that told him that all you have to do is work hard and be well liked to get to the top? Has the America that rewarded idealism now become an America that takes advantage of it, rewarding capitalism instead?

On the other hand, the play supports the idea that Willy, not society, is to blame for the great sadness in the Loman house. Miller has written a complex and subtle psychological portrait of a man with deep flaws in his character. In psychological terms, you could argue that because his father left him at the age of three, Willy suffers from an 'abandonment complex'. Willy's need for approval and admiration from all may be an attempt to redress an overwhelming feeling of worthlessness. He places great pressure on Biff to be the opposite of himself and has distaste for people who bear any similarity to him (such as Happy, Bernard, Charley). He co-opts his wife to maintain whatever fiction is required to preserve the illusion that he is someone who would never be abandoned. In this interpretation we can understand Linda's constant reframing of reality as an attempt to relieve the sufferings that began for Willy long before his fortunes as a salesman started to wane. Willy mythologises the family's early travels with his father, and Ben's travels later. The presence of his father's flute at the beginning and end resonates deeply, as does Willy's seemingly conflicting desire for Biff to have all the attributes of Ben and their father, but at the same time never wanting him to leave and go out West.

Q Is Willy a victim of events or did he bring them on himself? Is *Death of a Salesman* an indictment on the American Dream or an exploration of neurotic dysfunction? Or is it both?

Linda Loman

Key quotes

'Be loving to him. Because he's only a little boat looking for a harbour. [*She is trembling with sorrow and joy.*] Oh, that's wonderful, Biff, you'll save his life' (p.59).

'You're my foundation and my support, Linda' (Willy, p.13).

'Willy, dear, I can't cry. Why did you do it? I search and search and I search, and I can't understand it, Willy' (p.112).

Linda holds the fabric of the play's world together. Willy's wife is often seen as a 'conflicted character'. On one level she is the most rational force in the Loman household, actively managing Willy's psychological problems and his relationships while at the same time attending to the reality of day-to-day living (paying bills, organising maintenance, etc.). On the other, conflicting, level, Linda is also active in conflating Willy's already out-of-control delusions and pushing him further into an alternative version of reality that is destined to destroy itself as it collides with the real world.

Linda and Biff are the only characters who make explicit reference to Willy's delusions, but their positions are completely opposite to one another. Biff, who holds little emotional attachment to his father, believes he needs to be confronted with harsh reality to make him snap out of the delusions that imprison Linda and the whole family, while Linda believes that Willy needs to be cushioned from harsh reality to protect him from his suicidal tendencies.

Q Is Linda providing the right kind of foundation and support to her delusional, ailing husband?

Biff Loman

Key quotes

'I realized what a ridiculous lie my whole life has been. We've been talking in a dream for fifteen years' (p.82).

'I ran down eleven flights with a pen in my hand today. And suddenly I stopped, you hear me? And in the middle of that office building, do you hear this? I stopped in the middle of that building and I saw – the sky. I saw the things that I love in this world. The work and the food and time to sit and smoke. And I looked at the pen and said to myself, what the hell am I grabbing this for? Why am I trying to become what I don't want to be?' (pp.104–5).

'I'm not a leader of men, Willy, and neither are you … I'm one dollar an hour … I'm not bringing home any prizes any more, and you're going to stop waiting for me to bring them home!' (p.105).

> [Willy] wants to live on through something ... and in his case, his masterpiece is his son. (Miller, in Kakutani 1984)

Biff is Willy's favourite son, and serves as the focal point of all of Willy's dreams. The first time we hear about Biff, the portrait Willy paints is a negative one, describing him as a 'bum' (p.11). But whenever Willy retreats into the past, we see the opposite. Willy idolises his son with an intense passion, and praises his virtues to all and sundry. Somewhere in between both these extremely negative and extremely positive viewpoints lies the real Biff.

It is notable that Biff speaks plainly and honestly to all; he is certainly the only member of the Loman family who does not sugar-coat the truth. Like Willy, Biff is also a dramatic portrait of a man whose life took a false turn. In Willy's case it was abandonment by his father. In Biff's case it is being betrayed and lied to by his father. Unlike Willy, Biff recognises that he is not made for city life. Like his father, however, Biff also aspires to achieving the great American Dream, just an older, more rustic version of it – going out West and working hard with your hands.

Biff is presented as somebody capable of achieving whatever he desires but whose will to do so is destroyed by a particular incident in his life. When Biff catches his father having an affair, he discovers that his entire life has been built on a lie and he is no longer able to engage in the illusions that Linda and Happy partake in.

Biff can be seen as the most heroic figure in *Death of a Salesman* because he is the only one willing (or able) to grapple with the central dilemma of the play: the contrast between truth and fiction.

Biff's great challenge is to find a way of separating his sense of self-worth from his work life and from the expectations that his father has indoctrinated him with.

Happy Loman

Key quotes

'Sometimes I want to just rip my clothes off in the middle of the store and outbox that goddam merchandise manager. I mean I can outbox, outrun, and outlift anybody in that store, and I have to take orders from those common, petty sons-of-bitches till I can't stand it any more' (p.18).

'I gotta show some of those pompous, self-important executives over there that Hap Loman can make the grade. I want to walk into the store the way he walks in' (p.18).

'I'm gonna show you and everybody else that Willy Loman did not die in vain. He had a good dream. It's the only dream you can have – to come out number-one man. He fought it out here, and this is where I'm gonna win it for him' (p.111).

If Biff is the focal point of all of Willy's dreams of redemption then Willy's second son, Happy, is the opposite. Largely ignored or swept aside from the central action in the Loman family, Happy (unlike Biff) has never risen to any of life's challenges and has remained immersed in Willy's rose-coloured view of the world. Happy's behaviour can be seen as a distorted outcome of Willy's ideals: where Willy makes a big deal of the importance of physical attractiveness, Happy puts that into practice by pathologically seducing women; where Willy insists that being well liked is the key to success, Happy seeks attention and praise for the most mundane and trifling of acts (notice how many times Happy asks if Willy's noticed him losing weight, for example).

Happy is also willing to tell any kind of lie in the hope of being impressive: 'It's really Harold, but at West Point they called me Happy' (p.80). (West Point is America's most prestigious and elite officer training school – Happy didn't really attend.) As the character who wholeheartedly believed in Willy's constructed universe, Happy represents the fallout of a life of falsehood. In telling Miss Forsythe the lie about West Point, on a semiotic level, he is saying 'I am only *Happy* when I am in a false, invented world'.

Q At the beginning of the play Happy seems much less troubled than Biff, however, by the time we see him at the funeral, which character would you rather be – him or Biff?

Q How comforted are you by Happy's tragically deluded claim: 'He had a good dream ... the only dream you can have – to come out number one-man. He fought it out here, and this is where I'm gonna win it for him' (p.111)?

Charley

Key quotes

'Willy, when're you gonna realize that them things don't mean anything? You named him Howard, but you can't sell that. The only thing you got in this world is what you can sell. And the funny thing is that you're a salesman, and you don't know that' (pp.76–7).

'Nobody dast blame this man. You don't understand; Willy was a salesman. And for a salesman, there is no rock bottom to the life. He don't put a bolt to a nut, he don't tell you the law or give you medicine. He's man way out there in the blue, riding on a smile and a shoeshine' (p.111).

Charley, Willy's neighbour, long-time rival and grudging friend, usually appears at heightened points in the drama. Charley moderates Willy's more extreme behaviour and acts as a measuring stick against which we can judge just how far Willy's delusions extend. Like Linda, Charley finds himself on the receiving end of Willy's hostility. In many ways Charley represents the simple reality that Willy is trying to escape from. Charley doesn't seem to value anything that Willy holds in high regard, and often his mockery seems designed to moderate some of Willy's more extreme hopes and dreams. For example, he gently tries to guide Willy away from putting so much value on Biff's performance in football. Notice how Charley holds no stock in being liked, or being good at sport or admired by others, and yet is successful.

We can interpret much of the hostility between Willy and Charley as good-natured. There is evidence of warmth and genuine care between the two families: both Biff and Happy refer to Charley with the honorific term 'Uncle'. Charley is mostly oblivious to Willy's barrage of insults and mockery and when times get tough Charley is the only person that Willy feels that he can turn to for financial help. Bernard, Charley's son, also shows great warmth toward Willy.

Charley works hard to buffer Willy from the harsher results of his delusions. We see very early on that he is acutely aware of Willy's condition. Charley works on Willy in two ways; first, he gently downgrades some of his delusions of grandeur (for which he becomes the object of Willy's derision) and secondly he tries to provide Willy with alternative possibilities for the future (including going so far as to offer Willy a job at his firm).

It is necessary for Willy to mock Charley because Charley is a living embodiment of the fact that all of the things that Willy believes in are deluded and patently untrue. Charley recognises this and has the good grace to forgive Willy for it. Charley is also proof that Arthur Miller does not set out to criticise 'business' in general, because Charley, a businessman, is an overwhelmingly positive force in the play.

Bernard

Key quotes

'I've often thought how of strange it was that I knew he'd given up his life. What happened in Boston, Willy?' (p.74).

'But sometimes, Willy, it's better for a man just to walk away.' ... 'But if you can't walk away?' ... 'I guess that's when it's tough' (Bernard and Willy, p.75).

We meet two very different versions of Bernard in the play. In the first act the Bernard we meet is a projection from Willy's memories, a version Willy chooses to remember, whereas in Act Two we meet the real, adult Bernard. They differ in a number of key areas. The young, imaginary Bernard appears bookish and un-sporty; he also comes across as mildly irritating and barely tolerated by Willy's two athletic sons. This Bernard is also presented as a very weak candidate for success. The imaginary Bernard acts as an intrusion (possibly created by Willy's own subconscious) into Willy's imaginary world. This intrusive version of Bernard can be seen leading Willy to the truth that he has been trying to suppress.

When Willy meets the real Bernard he then becomes a catalyst for Willy's catastrophic realisation about Biff. This Bernard is the one who asks the key question that unlocks the mystery of Willy's delusions: 'What happened in Boston, Willy?' (p.74). Where Charley acts as a cushioning force for Willy, Bernard (in both versions) acts as the agency triggering Willy's realisation.

Ben

Key quotes

'William, when I walked into the jungle, I was seventeen. When I walked out I was twenty-one. And, by God, I was rich!' (pp.40–1).

'The jungle is dark but full of diamonds, Willy ... [*with greater force*] One must go in to fetch a diamond out' (p.106).

Willy's older brother Ben left for Alaska and found his fortune in Africa. Ben is a special character because he appears in *Death of a Salesman* entirely as a projection of Willy's imagination. Unlike Bernard, who appears as 'real' as well as imagined, we have nothing with which to compare Willy's imagined brother. Ben represents the apotheosis of success to Willy. The information we have about Ben is so scarce that it becomes mythic. We know that he entered the jungle at seventeen and came out four years later as a rich man but we are given no details about exactly what it was that he did. Ben seems to come from an earlier time, even than the flashbacks. He feels like a character from the late nineteenth century: an age that rewarded courage, enterprise and brute force.

Ben, as a product entirely of Willy's memory and imagination, gives us an insight into Willy's subconscious. Note that Ben nearly always appears when Willy is at his most distressed and that Willy never conflicts with Ben (because Ben is disconnected from the reality with which Willy is so at odds). Ben's mythic pronouncements provide comfort to Willy because Ben also exists as a father figure – notice Willy's great desire for approval from Ben, as well as his devotion to his ideals. Ben is always in a hurry to leave and has extremely limited time for Willy.

Miss Forsythe and Letta

Both girls are prostitutes. It may be difficult to determine this from the way Happy interacts with them, because his conversation with them is coded, but notice the way he gives them gentle orders and says to Biff, 'Do you want her? She's on call' (p.81), hinting that she is a 'callgirl'. Notice how comfortable Willy is in the company of people who falsify reality as a profession. The presence of sexually available women adds poignancy to Willy's flashback to when Biff accidentally caught his father with Miss Francis.

Relationships

As with the characters, the majority of the relationships in the play are based in struggle; they're in a fierce tug of war. Characters often want something they can't get from other characters, and at the base of it all is a fierce love. These characters, whether they say so or not, do love each other. That's what makes the struggle so painful.

Sons and fathers

Key quote

> 'Isn't that – isn't that remarkable? Biff – he likes me!' (Willy, p.106).

Willy and Biff, Willy and his father, Willy and Happy, Charley and Bernard: what sons think of their fathers and what fathers want for their sons is pivotal in the script. In the Loman family Willy is profoundly affected by the absence of his father, while Biff becomes overwhelmed with too much of a father figure in his life. Happy wants his father's attention so much, he *becomes* Willy. Comparatively, there is the relationship between Charley and Bernard: Willy is astonished that Charley 'never took any interest' in Bernard (p.75) and yet he becomes the most successful of the three boys.

Willy and Linda

Key quotes

'He's the dearest man in the world to me, and I won't have anyone making him feel unwanted and low and blue' (Linda, p.43).

'I won't have you mending stockings in this house!' (Willy, p.31).

Willy and Linda love each other and are there for each other. Linda is so supportive of Willy that she stands behind him even though she suspects his dreams are flawed. Willy despairs that Linda has 'suffered' (p.84). But neither Linda nor Willy tell the truth to each other. Willy has an affair, and tries to hide the money he gets from Charley. Linda won't stand up to Willy. The lack of truth coupled with undying love is a toxic mix for the pair.

Willy and Ben

Willy is obsessed with the seemingly instant and effortless success of his brother, Ben. Ben offered Willy a chance to go to Alaska, and Willy has regretted rejecting it all his life. Is Willy's memory of Ben real or an illusion? Ben is a fragment of a character, almost ghost-like as he wafts into the scenes. He's the only projected character who talks to the present day Willy, ultimately encouraging him to commit suicide by saying that one must go into the dark in order to 'fetch a diamond out' (p.106).

Willy and Charley

Willy spends the whole play insulting Charley, calling him stupid, believing himself the better, more successful man. In the end, Charley is the only person from whom Willy can borrow money when he's desperate, and he calls Charley his 'only friend' (p.77).

THEMES, IDEAS & VALUES

The American Dream

Key quotes

'What's the mystery? The man knew what he wanted and went out and got it! Walked into a jungle, and comes out, the age of twenty-one, and he's rich! The world is an oyster, but you don't crack it open on a mattress!' (Willy, p.32).

'I put thirty-four years into this firm ... You can't eat the orange and throw the peel away – a man is not a piece of fruit!' (p.64).

'Instead of the ideals of hard work and courage, we have salesmanship' (Clurman, in Weales 1996, p.212).

Arthur Miller once stated that every American writer was writing about the American Dream in some way because it is the dominant myth of the nation. *Death of a Salesman* is widely regarded as the first great play that offers serious critical insights into the American Dream. In its early stages in the seventeenth century, the American Dream was ideologically based, and centred around the idea that every human being has the right to live free of bondage and tyranny, and to access as much of the bounty of the earth as their toils and aptitude will allow. By the twenty-first century, however, the American Dream has undergone considerable modification as American society itself changes. Currently, one could argue that the American Dream centres around a desire to live free from terrorism, with adequate access to a comfortable living wage and fluid credit.

We meet the ageing Willy Loman in 1949: a point in time when the idea of the American Dream was undergoing a process of change. Evidence of different versions of the dream can be found in each of the men. Biff and Ben are both clear exponents of an old-fashioned version of the American Dream, one familiar to anyone who has seen 'cowboy' or 'Western' films. Both Biff and Ben believe in the old adage that to find opportunity and fortune all a man need do is 'go West' into the frontier territory to claim their birthright as free men through hard, physical work and determination.

Ben's version of this dream is the clearest – he makes a regular point of reciting a parable about himself that proves a man can make a fortune out of nothing but pure enterprise: 'William, when I walked into the jungle, I was seventeen. When I walked out I was twenty-one. And, by God, I was rich!' (pp.40–1). Ben is an advocate of what you could call 'old-school' American values. Notice how Willy is equally threatened and excited by the purity and single-minded drive of Ben's ideology and also how desperate Willy is to gain approval from Ben by attaching his sons and (perversely enough) life in Brooklyn to the idea of a life in the wilderness: 'It's Brooklyn, I know, but we hunt too ... there's snakes and rabbits and – that's why I moved out here' (p.39). Ben makes regular references to the 'wild' and to Loman men being 'wild-hearted'. There is a strong suggestion of a kind of birthright or sense of inheritance passed down from Willy's father to Ben, partially through Willy and finally to Biff.

Biff carries his own version of the American Dream that is similar to Ben's but notably different because he is caught between two dreams. There's the 'wilderness' dream (embodied by Ben), that is extreme and mythically distant, and requires a kind of jungle ruthlessness in order to get to the 'diamonds'; and the urban dream Willy has instilled in him – where easy success in business awaits any man who is physically attractive and 'well liked'. You can hear the internal conflict of these two ideals in Biff:

> There's nothing more inspiring or – beautiful than the sight of a mare and a new colt. And it's cool there now, see? Texas is cool now, and it's spring. And whenever spring comes to where I am, I suddenly get the feeling, my God, I'm not gettin' anywhere. What the hell am I doing, playing around with horses, twenty-eight dollars a week! I'm thirty-four years old, I oughta be makin' my future. That's when I come running home. (pp.16–17)

Throughout the play we witness Biff shaking off the last vestiges of 'the wrong dreams' (p.110) that his father taught him, and gravitating back to a simpler ideal of opportunity out in the fields. Biff knows that the dream his father bought into during the 1940s has been false, and he seems willing to fall back on a life of physical labour in order to find contentment within himself.

Willy's version of the American Dream is one of the primary concerns of the play. The key difference between Willy's postwar version and the eighteenth-century version of the dream is that Willy's is fundamentally urban, industrial and capitalist, whereas the older one was about adventure and the great outdoors. In Willy's version of the dream, an individual's success is reliant on external forces in the form of business and other people. With the commodities boom that followed the end of the Second World War, and the sudden rise in the fortunes of some Americans at the expense of others, this new urban version of the dream implied that success is directly proportionate to material wealth. Willy's somewhat warped idea is that the city resembles the old frontier of the American West because he believes that all a man needs to do for reward is work hard and be likeable. He doesn't realise that the rules have changed since the war and, for most working Americans, their labour now barely even guarantees a subsistence.

Abandonment

Key quotes

'No, Ben! Please tell about Dad. I want my boys to hear. I want them to know the kind of stock they spring from. All I remember is a man with a big beard, and I was in Mamma's lap, sitting around a fire, and some kind of high music' (Willy, pp.37–8).

'You're a pair of animals! Not one, not another living soul would have had the cruelty to walk out on that man in a restaurant!' (Linda, p.98).

An often overlooked but nevertheless very important theme in *Death of a Salesman* is that of abandonment. Much of the emotional and dramatic action can be traced to what could be described as Willy's 'abandonment complex'. First, Willy's father left his children and then Ben also abandoned Willy for Alaska.

In the absence of a father figure Willy has constructed a fantasy system that provides him with the sense of security and relevance that a father might have provided. Notice how Willy frequently struggles to gain admiration, acceptance and tangible proof of success. Notice also how he (like Happy) is very quick to adopt another viewpoint or version of reality and reject his own values if it will ensure that he will gain admiration and approval.

Willy's subconscious fear of abandonment intersects with the American Dream because it has caused him to create a fixed, inflexible version of it in order to establish what he thinks will be an ordered and stable universe. The only trouble is that much larger global economic forces are at work, making Willy's old dream irrelevant and unattainable. Willy makes reference to 'always being contradicted' (p.12) – this feeling arises because Willy's imaginary version of reality cannot tally with the 'real' reality. He is unwilling, or unable, to adapt to new circumstances because his fear of abandonment makes him grasp for the reality with which he feels most secure (his fantasy). Even the normally forgiving and tolerant Linda reacts harshly to Biff and Happy abandoning their father in Frank's Chop House (p.97).

Willy's overweening interest in the fortunes of his children and his investment in their future suggests a man desperate to recreate himself in the image of a perfect father, after the abandonment of his own imperfect father. Notice how comprehensive Willy's advice is to his sons and how important it is to him in his reminiscences that his sons idolise and dote on him.

Disillusionment

Key quote

'The man don't know who we are! The man is gonna know! ... We never told the truth for ten minutes in this house' (Biff, p.104).

Every member of the Loman family seems to be dealing with a catalogue of unrealised dreams and unfulfilled potential. We hear a good deal of proselytising (talking at great length, advocating) about outcomes and possibilities but there is very little actual action. A good example can be found in the amount of stage time dedicated to Biff's planned visit to Oliver, followed by the amount of talk generated after the visit. The act itself is not depicted in the play. Miller uses this device regularly, such as in Willy's build-up to visiting his boss, or in Ben's constant and almost circular references to his exploits. This is a play replete with things much talked about but rarely achieved, about goals desired but unattained, dreams dreamt but never realised, and what we hear from the Loman family is a dialogue of disillusionment – quite literally, all talk and no action.

The theme of disillusionment intersects with the theme of the great American Dream on a fundamental level. The Loman family's inability to attain the American Dream (neither Willy's urban industrial version nor Biff's old-fashioned version) is the wellspring for their disillusionment.

The term '*dis*illusionment' implies that at one time an illusion existed and was then somehow taken away. Miller suggests that when dreams are not realised, they are often replaced by new versions which allow the dreamer to pretend to themselves that the original dream was never lost. Notice, for example, how Willy reinterprets his dream of being the number one salesman in New England. Willy often refers to his perceived status as the most liked and successful salesman in his appointed area, that he was the Wagner company's 'New England man' (p.10). Evidence, however, points to the contrary, most notably, Willy (even as a younger man) was regularly unable to make enough commission to cover the costs of debt repayments and basic household costs. As a result of this mismatch between the dream and reality a new illusion is generated: Willy creates an illusion that New England is the toughest American state for a visiting salesman. Even though he is not doing well, he convinces himself that in comparison to all other salesmen he is still doing better, and that all he needs to do is go to areas where he is well liked: 'Oh, I'll knock 'em dead next week. I'll go to Hartford. I'm very well liked in Hartford' (p.28).

Another example of Willy's tendency to create substitute illusions is the way he alters his smaller fantasy systems quickly in order to protect his larger dreams from coming into catastrophic contact with reality. For example, he downgrades his professed earnings from a work trip as reality (in the form of Linda's questioning) asserts itself.

> **Willy:** I did five hundred gross in Providence and seven hundred gross in Boston.
>
> **Linda:** No! Wait a minute, I've got a pencil. [*She pulls pencil and paper out of her apron pocket.*] That makes your commission ... Two hundred – my God! Two hundred and twelve dollars!

> **Willy:** Well, I didn't figure it yet, but ...
>
> **Linda**: How much did you do?
>
> **Willy:** Well, I – I did – about a hundred and eighty gross in Providence. Well, no – it came to – roughly two hundred gross on the whole trip. (p.27)

Similarly, when he discovers that expensive car repairs need to be paid for, Willy jumps effortlessly from one illusion (the Studebaker is the finest automobile available) to another completely contrasting one (the sale of Studebakers should be illegal) in order to protect the main illusion that the family is in good financial shape. Substitute illusions happen on an emotional level too: at the end of the play, Willy manages to reinterpret Biff's breakdown (and the destruction of the family myth that the Lomans are anything better than ordinary) as a demonstration of Biff's affection and the illusion that he is still loved by his son: '[*after a long pause, astonished, elevated*] Isn't that – isn't that remarkable? Biff – he likes me!' (p.106).

This final substitute illusion exists on a much larger level than the others and is an example of a 'mythic consolation' (an excuse hidden within a highly complicated illusion). In a world like the one Willy Loman has built around himself, where reality and illusion are often indistinguishable from each other because the premise of both is regularly altered, it becomes possible to rearrange the very foundations of one's reason for being. There are a number of mythic consolations evident in *Death of a Salesman*. Note how Happy manages to re-interpret his version of the American Dream at the end of the play, to justify his inaction. Happy manages to convince himself (but perhaps no one else) that staying in his position as assistant to the assistant buyer is in fact a way of proving that Willy did not live his life in vain. This is an example of a substitute illusion so grand that it can be seen as a mythic consolation for one's entire life. Linda also takes part in mythic consolation by allowing herself to believe that by actively participating in Willy's accelerating delusions, she is actually saving his life.

Biff, perhaps the most disillusioned character in the play, does not participate in this highly advanced form of illusion substitution. As a result he is the only member of the family who we feel has a hope of breaking out of the dream/disillusionment/substitute delusion pattern.

The rise of materialism

Key quotes

'Why do you get American when I like Swiss? ... I don't want a change! I want Swiss cheese. Why am I always being contradicted?' (Willy, p.12).

'I hope we didn't get stuck on that machine.' ... 'They got the biggest ads of any of them!' (Willy and Linda, p.27).

When *Death of a Salesman* was written, the economic framework of America was in a state of transition from a wartime economy to a consumer economy, and the market was becoming flooded with consumer goods. A key indication that society was changing was that someone's 'conspicuous consumption' (what they were seen to be buying) indicated what level of success they were enjoying.

This new mentality manifests itself throughout *Death of a Salesman* in a number of ways. Perhaps most prominent is the way in which brand names and products become a part of everyday conversation. In theatre and literature before *Death of a Salesman*, there are few references to brand names. This is difficult to imagine in twenty-first-century Western capitalist society where brand names are an integral and essential part of our everyday language. In the late 1940s and early 1950s, however, this process was in its infancy. Have a close look at how often new products and brand names are mentioned in the play. The rise of materialism as a mechanism for evaluating one's sense of self-worth had become a new and powerful force by 1949.

Material goods are also referred to in this play in a way that highlights another key theme, that of our innate resistance to change: 'You can't see nothing out here! They boxed in the whole goddamn neighbourhood!' (Willy, p.101). Change is a very big part of *Death of a Salesman*; Willy's own dreams and aspirations signal a change in the focus of American society from ideals to consumerism and even his job acts as a symbol of that change. However, on a personal level, Willy seems to have a great deal of difficulty coping with the small exigencies of change. Notice how he falls into rages over the smallest symbols of change, like the emergence of a newfangled kind of whipped cheese (p.12) and the sense that he is in a race against the junkyard for ownership of his material goods:

> I just finished paying for the car and it's on its last legs. The refrigerator consumes belts like a goddam maniac. They time those things. They time them so when you finally paid for them, they're used up. (p.57)

Sub-themes

In addition to the major themes, a play as sophisticated as *Death of a Salesman* will also be replete with smaller (or 'sub') themes. Some are listed here but the list is far from exhaustive. See what evidence you can find to discuss some of the themes below, and challenge your analytical ability by detecting new themes and sub-themes embedded in this expansive text.

- The West, Alaska and the African jungle
- Heredity and family history
- Gender relations
- Pride
- Madness
- The dangers of nostalgia and remorse
- Infidelity
- Opportunity
- Visions of America
- Family mythmaking and its consequences
- Keeping up appearances

Motifs

Themes and dominant ideas in good plays are often backed up by ***motifs***: story elements that recur at specific times in the drama, often repeated in different contexts to reinforce or develop an emotional, intellectual or even subconscious idea. Motifs often serve as symbols as well. Many plays do not work on this level of sophistication, relying on the power of the story and dramatic action to carry all the information, but Arthur Miller is regarded as a master of motif and symbol. What makes Miller special among late-twentieth-century playwrights is the manner in which he is able to seamlessly integrate motif and symbol into his dramatic action. He manages to do it in a way that is embedded into the narrative; that is, the motifs are present but do not jump out at you or interrupt the flow of the drama.

Miller uses motifs in many different forms. Sometimes they are quite visible and explicit. This is the case for some of the more basic ideas that he is trying to reinforce, such as the notions of the wilderness and the jungle. These motifs help Miller suggest a theme of the emergence of a competitive, 'dog-eat-dog' culture in American society – a culture that echoes a time when humans were subject to the laws of the jungle. Diamonds and ivory often emerge as motifs in relation to the rewards available to those who have the gumption to subject themselves to the laws of the wilderness. At the end of the play, Ben says to Willy, of the jungle, 'One must go in to fetch a diamond out' (p.106). Throughout the play we have been gently introduced to the idea of diamonds as the reward for having to expose yourself to terrible dangers. When Ben says the line above to Willy – just at the point that he is deciding to commit suicide so his family will receive the insurance money – we know that the 'jungle' is suicide and the 'diamond' that Willy must fetch out is the insurance money.

Another simple motif that recurs throughout the play is that of gardens and the planting and growing of seeds. The idea of gardening is a symbolic parallel for the idea of raising a family, so through this motif we find ourselves associating ideas of gardening with Willy's own family – was enough weeding done? Did Willy give his boys fertile enough soil to plant their roots in? As with the jungle and diamond motifs, Miller follows through with the gardening motif, and it reaches its climax when Willy is abandoned by his own sons at Frank's Chop House. Willy asks the waiter, 'is there a seed store in the neighbourhood?' (p.96), and the implication is that Willy feels the need to start again with his family. The waiter's answer, through this symbolism, becomes all the more poignant: 'Well, there's hardware stores on Sixth Avenue, but it may be too late now' (p.96).

Arthur Miller also uses motif in another complex way: using a dramatic state or a character's feelings as a motif. A good example of this technique can be found in his development of the feeling of being 'used up' (p.57) or worn out and discarded. References to these feelings include Willy's complaints about consumer goods, his references to being tired and worn out, his unwillingness to replace obsolete things and his reference to his own life: 'You can't eat the orange and throw the peel away – a man is not a piece of fruit!' (p.64). The motif is reinforced so well that by the time Willy throws his own life away, it seems as though his attitude has become a self-fulfilling prophecy. Willy has come to see himself in a similar way to how society sees consumable goods. The motif of being used up and discarded becomes an action in the drama, and works equally well as a powerful plot point and an affecting emotional metaphor.

Miller is as sophisticated on the level of motif and symbolism as he is on broader thematic ideas. Below is a list of some motifs to look out for, but the list is by no means exhaustive. Once again challenge yourself to find as many recurring and reinforced symbols and ideas as you can.

- Being 'indoors' and being 'outdoors'. Think about the deeper meaning in lines like 'Gotta break your neck to see a star in this yard' (p.41). Note how Miller makes use of this motif and couples it with the symbols of the moon and the stars.
- Attractiveness and good looks. Good looks are constantly reinforced as panacea (a universal key to most problems). See if you can trace where this imagined power loses its currency.
- Sexual conquests. Notice how Willy and Happy have a similar way of sexualising women and how Biff is referred to as having lost his touch: 'Where's ... the old confidence?' (p.15). How does

this motif affect your understanding of the internal masculinity and moral framework of these men? What does it do to your instinctual reaction to Linda?

- Childishness. Characters regularly use childish language like 'gee whiz' around Willy, and call him 'kid'. Notice also how Biff describes himself as a 'boy'. How does this motif contribute to the themes of the play?

DIFFERENT INTERPRETATIONS

Different interpretations arise from different responses to a text. Over time, a text will evoke a wide range of responses from its readers, who may come from various social or cultural groups and live in very different places and historical periods. Responses by critics and reviewers can be published in newspapers, journals and books, or they can be expressed in discussions among readers in the media, classrooms, book groups and so on. While there is no single correct reading or interpretation of a text, it is important to understand that an interpretation is more than a personal opinion – it is the justification of a point of view on the text. To present an interpretation of the text based on your point of view you must use a logical argument and support it with relevant evidence from the text.

Death of a Salesman opened at the Morosco Theatre on Broadway in New York in 1949, directed by Elia Kazan. It was instantly well received and its first season ran for 742 performances. The first critical responses were overwhelmingly positive and the piece went on to win Tony Awards for Best Play, Author, Director, Supporting Actor, Set Design and Producer. The play also garnered many other prestigious awards such as the New York Drama Critics' Circle Award and the Pulitzer Prize.

New York theatre critics are rarely unanimous in their praise, and even with the most well-received plays it is common to find a dissenting voice among critics (especially early in a play's life before a consensus sets in). The most common form of negative response to *Death of a Salesman* did not come from theatre critics, but from journalists, cultural commentators and politicians who were alarmed by the great success of a play that seemed to be critical of American capitalist society at a time when the nation was in the grip of a cold war with its Communist enemy, the USSR. This criticism was of a political nature and has little impact on our reception of the play's qualities as a work of art. The play is still regularly performed to great acclaim – for example, a 2011 Broadway production was directed by Mike Nichols and starred Phillip Seymour Hoffman as Willy.

The excerpts that follow are examples of the first critical responses (from a document compiled by Michael Lupu for the Guthrie Theater's 2004 production).

- 'A great play of our day has opened at the Morosco. *Death of a Salesman*, by Arthur Miller, has majesty, sweep and shattering dramatic impact ... There is always pertinence to this tale of a defeated old drummer coming to the dead end of his career. A terrible documentation has been leavened with bursts of wild humor and more than one moment of touching grandeur, while the fluent scenes build inexorably to the climax ... The offering is theater of the first order' (Howard Barnes, *Herald Tribune*).
- 'In Arthur Miller's Salesman there's much of Everyman. Bothered, bewildered, but mostly bedeviled, as Willy Loman is, he's not a great deal different from the majority of his contemporaries. He, even as you and I, builds himself a shaky shelter of illusion ... Willy has created an image of himself which fails to correspond with Willy Loman as he is. According to the playwright, it's the size of the discrepancy that matters. In Salesman Loman, the discrepancy is so great that it finally slays him. Ironically, by his own unsteady hand' (Robert Garland, *The New York Journal American*).
- 'From every point of view, *Death of a Salesman* ... is a rich and memorable drama. It is so simple in style and so inevitable in theme that it scarcely seems like a thing that has been written and acted. For Mr Miller has looked with compassion into the hearts of some ordinary Americans and quietly transferred their hope and anguish to the theater ... *Death of a Salesman* has the flow and spontaneity of a suburban epic that may not be intended as poetry but becomes poetry in spite of itself ... Writing like a man who understands people, Mr Miller has no moral precepts to offer and no solutions of the salesman's problems. He is full of pity, but he brings no piety to it' (Brooks Atkinson, *The New York Times*).
- 'Mr Miller has been praised before for the "naturalness" of his dialogue. His writing in *Death of a Salesman* is splendid – terse, always in character and always aimed toward the furtherance of his drama' (John Chaplan, *Daily News*).

- Willy Loman 'has lived on his smile and on his hopes; survived from sale to sale; been sustained by the illusion that he has countless friends in his territory, that everything will be all right, that he is a success, and that his boys will be successes also. His misfortune is that he has gone through life as an eternal adolescent, as someone who has not dared to take stock, as someone who never knew who he was' (John Mason Brown, *Saturday Review of Literature*).
- 'The death of Arthur Miller's salesman is symbolic of the breakdown of the whole concept of salesmanship inherent in our society.
- Miller does not say these things explicitly. But it is the strength of the play that it is based on this understanding, and that he is able to make his audience realize it no matter whether or not they are able consciously to formulate it. When the audience weeps at *Death of a Salesman*, it is not so much over the fate of Willy Loman – Miller's pathetic hero – but over the millions of such men who are our brothers, uncles, cousins, neighbours ... Willy Loman never acknowledges or learns the error of his way. To the very end he is a devout believer in the ideology that destroys him. He believes that life's problems are solved by making oneself "well liked" (in the salesman's sense) and by a little cash' (Harold Clurman, *Tomorrow*).

Two interpretations

In the case of Arthur Miller's *Death of a Salesman* the two most common critical perspectives revolve around the root cause of the tragedy. On one level you can argue that Willy Loman is a victim of the social and economic forces around him or, on another, you could argue that Willy's own personal internal failings as a human being have brought about his tragic predicament. The first reading views the play as social commentary, the second views it from a psychological perspective.

1. *Death of a Salesman* argues that a rapidly changing society is to blame for Willy and the Lomans' unhappiness.

Death of a Salesman was written at a time of great economic and social change. It was a time when the 'American Dream' changed from one driven by ideals to one driven by money. Willy Loman is a man caught between these two conflicting versions of the American Dream – a man desperately trying to cling to the values of the past in a present that no longer values him. Willy Loman's tragedy is caused by the fact that American society no longer rewards the efforts of everyday working-class people.

At the time Arthur Miller wrote *Death of a Salesman* – only four years after the end of the Second World War – America had transformed itself into a highly industrialised society. When the war ended in 1945, instead of sending all of those industrial goods overseas, America sold them back to its own citizens. This created a commodities boom, which made some people very rich. However, it benefited a very small part of the population (investors) at the expense of most of the population (workers). It spelled the end of an America where opportunity was available to anyone keen enough to go out take it, and the start of an America where happiness was measured by material wealth. *Death of a Salesman* is a portrait of an American family left stranded by this sudden social and economic change.

Miller paints a portrait of an American family stuck in the past and running out of enthusiasm in the face of a bleak future. The Loman family are living a version of the prewar dream that is fading fast. The opening image of the play is a picture of an old-fashioned living arrangement; the stage directions describe *'a small, fragile-seeming home'* surrounded by *'towering, angular shapes'* (p.7) – the shapes of brand new apartment blocks. The first time we see the play's hero he is literally weighed down with baggage, his *'exhaustion is apparent'* (p.8) and the whole setting has the sense of *'a dream rising out of reality'* (p.7). To add to the sense of a family reluctant to let go of the past, Willy and Linda's two sons upstairs in their childhood bedrooms are now in their thirties.

The play abounds with evidence of a family clinging to a fading dream in the face of a rapidly arriving new order. Perhaps most potent is the way in which Miller artfully switches between an idealised past and a bleak and unhappy present. Willy's changes in mood occur explicitly with shifts in time. In the present he refers to his eldest son Biff as a 'bum' (p.11) but in the past calls him 'a young god' (p.54). As the play progresses and Willy's dreams of the past become less stable, so does his character.

Miller regularly references the arrival of new commodities in the play and each new item brings an added unhappiness to Willy. Early on, Linda's innocent conversation about a 'new kind of ... cheese' (p.12) triggers a violent outburst from Willy: 'I don't want a change ... why am

I always being contradicted?' (p.12). This follows a pattern of agitation triggered by new consumables – from refrigerators to cars – that rises throughout the play. Miller's subtle use of consumer goods to indicate the change in social circumstances is at its most poignant when we see the ageing salesman begging to keep his job, with his young boss Howard more interested in a new gadget (a tape recorder) than in the welfare of a long-time employee (pp.59–61).

Another way that Miller presents his argument of a new America rising up to swallow the old one is in his references to the encroachment of city life onto country life. Very early in the play Willy complains that his house in Brooklyn has become 'boxed ... in' and Linda says it once felt like they lived 'a million miles from the city' (p.12). In another instance Willy complains: 'Gotta break your neck to see a star in this yard' (p.41).

Perhaps the most poetic and powerful way in which Miller presents his argument of a family trapped in the past, unable to make the transition to the new version of the American Dream, is through Ben and Biff, who both represent pure versions of the idea that happiness exists outside the city lines. Ben's is a highly idealised version that exists solely in the distant past, typified by his refrain 'Why boys, when I was seventeen I walked into the jungle, and when I was twenty-one I walked out. And by God I was rich' (p.37), while Biff's is downgraded to meet the present possibility of merely becoming a farm labourer. Biff shatters his father's last hope of living the old American dream when he tells him:

> You were never anything but a hard-working drummer who landed in the ash-can like all the rest of them. I'm one dollar an hour ... I'm not bringing home any prizes any more, and you're going to stop waiting for me to bring them home! (p.105)

There are two different versions of the American Dream at play in *Death of a Salesman*: the one before the Second World War (the prewar dream), characterised by the belief that anybody with enough enthusiasm can find happiness in America, and the one after the Second World War where happiness and opportunity became defined by one's ability to buy and sell (the postwar dream). Willy Loman is a hardworking man whose happiness is dictated by extreme social and economic forces.

2. In the modern tragedy *Death of a Salesman*, Willy's personality flaws bring about his own downfall.

A tragedy is a drama in which the main character is brought to ruin or suffers extreme sorrow as a consequence of a tragic flaw. Arthur Miller's tragedy *Death of a Salesman* is a psychological portrait of a man with such a flaw; specifically, he suffers from what would now be termed a *narcissistic personality disorder*.

The clinical definition of narcissistic personality disorder fits very closely with Willy Loman's behaviour: the sufferer 'possesses a grandiose view of the self but has a conflict-ridden psychological dependence on others' (*Diagnostic and Statistical Manual of Mental Disorders*). This reading will match the nine classic symptoms of the disorder to demonstrate how Arthur Miller has presented us with an extraordinarily accurate portrait of a man suffering from a mental illness.

In order to be diagnosed with narcissistic personality disorder, the sufferer must fit five or more of the following nine descriptions (as set out by the diagnostic manual). Following each of the criteria, I have provided textual examples of the behaviours.

1 Has a grandiose sense of self-importance:

- '[... *in an uncontrolled outburst*] I am not a dime a dozen! I am Willy Loman, and you are Biff Loman!' (Willy, p.105).

2 Lives in a dream world of exceptional success:

- 'They don't need me in New York. I'm the New England man. I'm vital in New England' (Willy, p.10).
- 'Loves me. [*Wonderingly*.] Always loved me. Isn't that a remarkable thing? Ben, he'll worship me for it!' (Willy, p.107).

3 Thinks of himself/herself as 'special' or privileged:

- 'I never have to wait in line to see a buyer. "Willy Loman is here!" That's all they have to know, and I go right through' (Willy, p.26).

4 Demands excessive amounts of praise or admiration from others:

- Biff: Did you knock them dead Pop?

  Willy: Knocked 'em cold in Providence, slaughtered 'em in Boston (p.26).

- Willy: ... Now pay attention ... in 1928 I had a big year. I averaged a hundred and seventy dollars a week in commissions.

  Howard: [*impatiently*] Now, Willy, you never averaged –

  Willy: [*banging his hand on the desk*]: I averaged a hundred and seventy dollars a week in the year of 1928! (p.64).

5 Feels entitled to automatic deference or favourable treatment from others:

- 'The finest people. And when I bring you fellas up, there'll be open sesame for all of us, 'cause one thing, boys: I have friends. I can park my car in any street in New England, and the cops protect it like their own' (Willy, p.24).

6 Is exploitative towards others and takes advantage of them:

- 'Charley, look ... [*With difficulty.*] I got my insurance to pay. If you can manage it – I need a hundred and ten dollars' (Willy, p.75).

7 Lacks empathy and does not recognise or identify with others' feelings:

- Willy: They have office boys for that.

  Linda: I'll make a big breakfast –

  Willy: Will you let me finish? [*To* Biff.] Tell him you were in the business in the West (p.53).

8 Frequently envious of others or thinks that they are envious of him or her:

- Charley: What're you, jealous of me?

  Willy: I can't work for you, that's all, don't ask me why.

  Charley [*angered, takes out more bills*]: You been jealous of me all your life, you damned fool! Here, pay your insurance (p.77).

9 Frequently acts in haughty or arrogant ways:

- Charley: You're insulted again.

  Willy: A man who can't handle tools is not a man.
  You're disgusting (p.34).

QUESTIONS & ANSWERS

This section focuses on your own analytical writing on the text, and gives you strategies for producing high quality responses in your coursework and exam essays.

Essay writing – an overview

An essay is a formal and serious piece of writing that presents your point of view on the text, usually in response to a given essay topic. Your 'point of view' in an essay is your interpretation of the meaning of the text's language, structure, characters, situations and events, supported by detailed analysis of textual evidence.

Analyse – don't summarise

In your essays it is important to avoid simply summarising what happens in a text:

- A **summary** is a description or paraphrase (retelling in different words) of the characters and events. For example: 'Macbeth has a horrifying vision of a dagger dripping with blood before he goes to murder King Duncan'.
- An **analysis** is an explanation of the real meaning or significance that lies 'beneath' the text's words (and images, for a film). For example: 'Macbeth's vision of a bloody dagger shows how deeply uneasy he is about the violent act he is contemplating – as well as his sense that supernatural forces are impelling him to act'.

A limited amount of summary is sometimes necessary to let your reader know which part of the text you wish to discuss. However, always keep this to a minimum and follow it immediately with your analysis of what this part of the text is really telling us.

Plan your essay

Carefully plan your essay so that you have a clear idea of what you are going to say. The plan ensures that your ideas flow logically, that your argument remains consistent and that you stay on the topic. An essay plan should be a list of **brief dot points** – no more than half a page.

- Include your central argument or main contention – a concise statement of your overall response to the topic.
- Write three or four dot points for each paragraph, indicating the main idea and evidence/examples from the text. Note that in your essay you will need to expand on these points and analyse the evidence.

Structure your essay

An essay is a complete, self-contained piece of writing. It has a clear beginning (the introduction), middle (several body paragraphs) and end (the last paragraph or conclusion). It must also have a central argument that runs throughout, linking each paragraph to form a coherent whole.

See examples of introductions and conclusions in the 'Analysing a sample topic' and 'Sample answer' sections.

The introduction establishes your overall response to the topic. It includes your main contention and outlines the main evidence you will refer to in the course of the essay. Write your introduction after you have done a plan and before you write the rest of the essay.

The body paragraphs argue your case – they present evidence from the text and explain how this evidence supports your argument. Each body paragraph needs:

- a strong **topic sentence** (usually the first sentence) that states the main point being made in the paragraph;
- **evidence** from the text, including some brief quotations;
- **analysis** of the textual evidence explaining its significance and **explanation** of how it supports your argument;
- **links back** to the topic in one or more statements, usually towards the end of the paragraph.

Connect the body paragraphs so that your discussion flows smoothly. Use some linking words and phrases like 'similarly' and 'on the other hand', though don't start every paragraph like this. Another strategy is to use a significant word from the last sentence of a paragraph in the first sentence of the next.

Use key terms from the topic – or synonyms for them – throughout, so the relevance of your discussion to the topic is always clear.

The conclusion ties everything together and finishes the essay. It includes strong statements that emphasise your central argument and provide a clear response to the topic.

Avoid simply restating the points made earlier in the essay – this will end on a very flat note and imply that you have run out of ideas and vocabulary. The conclusion is meant to be a logical extension of what you have written, not just a repetition or summary. Writing an effective conclusion can be a challenge. Try using these tips:

- Start by linking back to the final sentence of the second-last paragraph – this helps your writing to 'flow', rather than just leaping back to your main contention straight away.
- Use synonyms and expressions with equivalent meanings to vary your vocabulary. This allows you to reinforce your line of argument without being repetitive.
- When planning your essay, think of one or two broad statements or observations about the text's wider meaning. These should be related to the topic and your overall argument. Keep them for the conclusion, since they will give you something 'new' to say but still follow logically from your discussion. The introduction will be focused on the topic, but the conclusion can present a wider view of the text.

Essay topics

1 Identify and discuss the causes of conflict between Willy and his son Biff.

2 Willy seems to long for the 'good old days'. What changes have happened in American society that bring him such unhappiness?

3 Do you think that consumerism promises more than it delivers? Are Americans better off now than they were in 1949? Why or why not?

4 Do you believe that Linda does the right thing by allowing Willy to live in a fantasy for so long? Identify the benefits and the failings in her decision.

5 Is *Death of a Salesman* a tragedy?

6 *Death of a Salesman* concludes with what is described as a 'Requiem'. What does Miller achieve by adding it to the play?

7 Biff is sometimes referred to as lazy, but at other times he is seen in a very positive light. Is he a positive or negative force within the play?

8 Willy Loman's personal hero, the almost mythical salesman Dave Singleman, died the 'death of a salesman' at age eighty-four. What does Willy mean by this description, and how does Dave Singleman's death differ from Willy's own?

9 There are a number of striking similarities between the world of the play and Arthur Miller's own life. Pinpoint the major similarities: how might Miller's own experience have helped shape the content of *Death of a Salesman*, and developed particular themes?

10 In the Requiem, Biff says that Willy had 'the wrong dreams'. What do you think 'the right dreams' could be, and how might they have helped Willy achieve success?

Useful vocabulary for writing on *Death of a Salesman*

Capitalism: An economic system based on the private ownership and purchase of property.

Catharsis: A release of emotional tension, as after an overwhelming experience; ***Cathartic realisation:*** A moment in a tragedy when the main protagonist sees the error of his ways (but is usually too late to fix it).

Consumerism: The theory that an increasing consumption of goods is beneficial.

Demotic language: Language that sounds like it is spoken naturally by common people of the time.

Expressionism: A form of art that places the greatest amount of emphasis on one's inner experience.

Genre: In a literary and dramatic sense, genre refers to a body of work that shares similarities in structure, language or subject matter.

Idealism: The act or philosophical pursuit of envisioning things in an ideal or perfect form.

Marxism: The economic and political theories of Karl Marx and Friedrich Engels that human actions and institutions are economically determined; that class struggle is needed to create historical change; and that capitalism will ultimately be superseded.

Materialism: A desire for wealth and material possessions with little interest in ethical or spiritual matters

Metaphor: When one thing is used to represent another; for example, Willy's garden can be seen as a metaphor for his family.

Mixed reality: When a dramatist deliberately breaks the unity of time and place within any given scene so that different times and places happen simultaneously on stage.

Motif: A recurrent image, word, phrase, theme, character or situation.

Realism: A form of art that sets out to represent real life as closely as possible; ***Social realism*** is a form of realism that attempts to explore the broader context of society.

Requiem: A song or prayer dedicated to someone who has died.

Symbolism: The practice of representing things by attributing meaning or significance (beyond the literal) to objects, events or relationships.

The Cold War: A state of political conflict using means that stop short of armed warfare, in this case between America and the USSR (Soviet Union).

Tragedy: A theatrical form in which a central protagonist comes to a downfall as a result of flaws in his/her character; ***American Tragedy*** is a form of tragedy in which the central character is placed at the mercy of forces in modern American society. The central character in American tragedy rarely comes to an understanding of the explicit reason for their fall.

Analysing a sample topic

Is *Death of a Salesman* a tragedy?

Begin your analysis by making a decision about what the terms in the topic mean and making sure that you fully understand the question. In this case the key would be your understanding of the term 'tragedy'. As there are many definitions (and opinions) as to what constitutes a tragedy you will have to find the one that you have the strongest opinion about.

For example, Aristotle's definition of a tragedy – 'the imitation of an action that is serious and also, as having magnitude, complete in itself incorporating incidents arousing pity and fear, wherewith to accomplish the catharsis of such emotions' – would offer you a comfortable framework for answering 'yes' to the question. If, however, you take your definition of tragedy as 'the circumstances that bring about the fall of a great man', you could argue 'no' on the basis that the central protagonist is not 'a great man'.

Let's presume that you will argue that the play is a tragedy. Once you have defined the key terms in the question and have formed a main contention, the next step is to interpret the 'framing' of the question. In this case the question is framed: 'Is *Death of a Salesman* a tragedy?' which implies you could argue one way or the other. If the topic was framed differently, for example, '*Death of a Salesman* is not a tragedy. Discuss.' then you might be more limited to a single position on the topic (although if your argument was strongly supported with evidence from the text, you could still disagree with the statement in your discussion).

Introductory paragraph

> If we adopt Aristotle's definition of tragedy as 'the imitation of an action that is serious and also, as having magnitude, complete in itself incorporating incidents arousing pity and fear, wherewith to accomplish the catharsis of such emotions', Arthur Miller's *Death of a Salesman* is certainly a tragedy, as it satisfies all the key areas of the definition. The play's primary focus is the internal life of a man in great distress but the story also functions as a grand metaphor for fundamental shifts occurring in the American Dream and American society as a whole.

Second paragraph: Does the play imitate 'an action that is serious'?

- Outline the action that is serious, e.g. '*Death of a Salesman* follows the final days of a man desperately trying to match the height of his dreams with the depths of his reality, and this functions as a metaphor for the plight of most ordinary Americans.'

- Give examples where small actions can be seen to represent a much larger story. For example, Mr Wagner's tape recorder – which Willy cannot operate – is a symbol of our inability to keep up with change.

Third paragraph: Does it have 'magnitude'?

- Find key examples where Miller uses individual experience as metaphor for society at large – for example, what does Willy's suicide represent on a broader social level?
- Demonstrate how Miller renders individual experience and emotion 'epic' (surpassing the ordinary, especially in size or scale).
- Show how the large-scale economic factors impact directly on the Lomans and their American Dream, and how the family functions as metaphor for American society.

Fourth paragraph: Does it 'arouse pity and fear'?

- Discuss the emotional impact of the play and techniques Miller uses to accomplish this.
- Demonstrate the use of language to trigger emotional responses, for example, 'he's only a little boat looking for a harbour' (p.59).
- Show how Miller gives us multiple viewpoints on a character by having his condition continually observed and discussed.
- Explain how the flashbacks and mixed reality offer us a sympathetic understanding of Willy Loman's personal experience.

Fifth paragraph: Does it 'accomplish a catharsis of such emotions'?

- Define 'catharsis' (a release of emotional tension, as after an overwhelming experience).
- Outline how catharsis occurs in the play, perhaps referencing several characters' different experiences to strengthen the argument.

Conclusion

Death of a Salesman satisfies the criteria in Aristotle's definition of tragedy, specifically that its action is 'serious', has 'magnitude' and arouses 'pity and fear' in order to achieve a 'catharsis'. The themes of personal misfortune ending in suicide and the seismic shifts in the American Dream are topics of 'magnitude' on both individual and national levels, and Miller uses dramatic techniques to trigger empathetic 'pity and fear' in his audience. Finally, Miller provides the audience with a framework to understand the fate of Willy Loman through catharsis. *Death of a Salesman* is certainly a tragedy, dealing with the misfortune that besets a man who functions as a metaphor for American society. It shows how changes in American society put great pressure on its people and therefore its central dream. *Death of a Salesman* is not only a tragedy, but the first great American tragedy.

SAMPLE ANSWER

***Death of a Salesman* concludes with what is described as a 'Requiem'. What does Miller achieve by adding it to the play?**

A 'requiem' is a song delivered in a religious ceremony to honour someone of importance who has died. The final scene of *Death of a Salesman* is not technically a requiem but carries all the attendant associations of one. On a dramaturgical level the scene would be more correctly described as an epilogue that carries the energy, tone and grandeur of a requiem. An epilogue is a traditional component to a play where the audience is addressed directly following the conclusion of a drama. Epilogues condense, clarify and conclude the governing arguments of the play. By imbuing his epilogue with the qualities of a requiem Arthur Miller succeeds in elevating the final moments of the play to an epic level while eloquently outlining the key argument of the play and maintaining a very personal, elegiac tone.

The requiem establishes dramatic rules that are very different to the rest of the play and it functions effectively as an epilogue, with added extras. Linda moves from the Loman's kitchen (the place where the majority of the dramatic action has taken place), and steps through the notional 'walls' of the house, and then Biff, Happy, Charley and Bernard join her and walk to 'the limit of the apron'. The majority of what follows is delivered directly to the audience in a 'mixed reality': part eulogy, part epilogue and part conventional dramatic scene. By creating this framework Miller is able to address all elements of the play within a very powerful context.

Requiems are usually delivered for people of importance and it is ironic that Willy receives one at all. Miller uses strong dramatic irony to frame discussion about a series of ironies that surrounded Willy's life. The first is that Willy's funeral is very poorly attended, despite the grandeur he had previously predicted for this event, and Linda expresses confusion at this, saying 'Why did nobody come?' This allows us to see that she has still not set herself free from some of the delusions and fantasies in which Willy cloaked the family. We discover that Willy was in fact financially 'free and clear' at the point when he decided to kill himself.

Throughout the play we have been presented with a catalogue of fantasies and delusions that have reaped malignant rewards but for the first time we witness a benign illusion. Charley allows the falsehood that the event is much grander than it actually is. He chooses to frame his eulogy to Willy in the most majestic terms available using a faux form of grand English – 'Nobody dast blame this man' – and engaging in poetic language that elevates the otherwise bleak and depressing context. What we are witnessing is a benign kind of fantasising, as Charley imagines Willy as 'a man way out there in the blue, riding on a smile and a shoeshine'.

By framing the epilogue as a requiem, Miller also provides a platform from which his characters have a chance to form a consensus on Willy's tragic condition. Until this moment each character is compelled to remain complicit with Willy's delusions (though to differing degrees) with the result that it is impossible to tell what each character truly feels. A key example of the change is the new consensus that Willy was unsuited to the work that he had raised to a mythic level:

> **Biff:** There were a lot of nice days. When he'd come home from a trip; or on Sundays, making the stoop; finishing the cellar; putting on the new porch; when he built the extra bathroom; and put up the garage. You know something, Charley, there's more of him in that front stoop than in all the sales he ever made.
>
> **Charley:** Yeah. He was a happy man with a batch of cement.
>
> **Linda:** He was so wonderful with his hands.

There is no consensus, however, on the root cause of Willy's tragedy. Biff declares that Willy believed in 'the wrong dreams' and 'didn't know who he was'. Happy disagrees and vows (ominously) to follow in his father's footsteps to prove his dreams were not false. Linda is left confused, unable to understand Willy's decision to kill himself. She focuses on their financial situation without being able to divine that it was in fact Willy's wilful manipulation of the truth, and the conflict this caused in his life, that was the cause of his downfall.

Ultimately, by using the form of a requiem Miller is able to engage in a dramatic irony that enhances the emotional tone of the play while delivering a final epilogue that effectively condenses, clarifies and concludes the argument of the play. By framing Willy's graveside scene as an illusion of a grand requiem, the last moments of *Death of a Salesman* show the Lomans and their neighbours engaging in one final departure from reality as they pay their respects to a man whose own reality was always filled with illusion.

REFERENCES & READING

Text

Miller, Arthur 1949, *Death of a Salesman*, Penguin, London.

References

Bentley, Eric 1953, *In Search of Theatre*, Knopf, New York.

Bigsby, Christopher (ed.) 1997, *The Cambridge Companion to Arthur Miller*, Cambridge University Press, New York.

Bloom, Harold (ed.) 2006, *Arthur Miller: Modern Critical Interpretations*, Chelsea House Publishing, New York.

Clurman, Harold (ed.) 1971, *The Portable Arthur Miller*, Viking, New York.

Diagnostic and Statistical Manual of Mental Disorders, Encyclopaedia of Mental Disorders, http://www.minddisorders.com/Kau-Nu/Narcissistic-personality-disorder.html

Eyre, Richard 2003, *Greatest Living Playwright: Arthur Miller*, WhatsOnStage.com, http://www.whatsonstage.com/features/theatre/london/E8821062866601/Greatest+Living+Playwright%3A+Arthur+Miller.html

Gassner, John 1954, *The Theatre in Our Times*, Crown, New York.

Hogan, Robert 1964, *Arthur Miller*, 'Pamphlets on American Writers', No. 40, University of Minnesota Press, Minneapolis.

Kakutani, Michiko 1984, 'Arthur Miller: View of a life', *The New York Times*, 9 May, http://www.nytimes.com/books/00/11/12/specials/miller-interview84.html?_r=2

Koon, Helene Wickham (ed.) 1983, *Twentieth Century Interpretations of Death of a Salesman: A Collection of Critical Essays*, Prentice-Hall, Englewood Cliffs.

Lupu, Michael 2004, *Death of a Salesman: A Study Guide*, Guthrie Theater, http://www.guthrietheater.org/sites/default/files/salesman.pdf

Murphy, Brenda 1995, *Miller: Death of a Salesman*, Plays in Production, Cambridge University Press, New York.

Martin, Robert A. (ed.) 1978, *The Theater Essays of Arthur Miller*, Viking, New York.

Miller, Arthur 1950, 'The "Salesman" has a birthday', *The New York Times*, 5 February, http://www.nytimes.com/books/00/11/12/specials/miller-birthsales.html

——1953, *The Crucible*, Penguin, London.

——1978, *Timebends: A Life*, Penguin, New York.

Roudané, Matthew C. 1987, *Conversations with Arthur Miller*, University Press of Mississippi, Jackson.

Tynan, Kenneth 1961, *Curtains*, Atheneum, New York, pp.257–66.

Weales, Gerald (ed.) 1996, *Death of a Salesman: Text and Criticism*, Penguin, New York.

Welland, Dennis 1961, *Arthur Miller*, Grove Press, New York.